God In Life

Anthology

Press Service International Writers

God In Life
Copyright © 2020 Star Label Publishing

Published by Star Label Publishing
P.O. Box 1511, Buderim, QLD, Australia
publishing@starlabel.com.au
Concept, compilation, cover art and design: Tony R Moore
Editor and Interior: Rebecca Moore; Editor: David Goodwin

1st Edition May, 2020
All rights reserved. No part of this publication may be reproduced in any form; stored in a retrieval system; or transmitted; or used in any other form; or by any other means without prior written permission of the publisher (except for brief quotes for the purpose of review or promotion).

Scripture quotations marked (ESV) are from The Holy Bible, English Standard Version® (ESV®), copyright © 2001 by Crossway, a publishing ministry of Good News Publishers. Used by permission. All rights reserved.

Scripture quotations marked (NIV) are taken from the Holy Bible, New International Version®, NIV®. Copyright © 1973, 1978, 1984, 2011 by Biblica, Inc.™ Used by permission of Zondervan. All rights reserved worldwide. www.zondervan.com. The "NIV" and "New International Version" are trademarks registered in the United States Patent and Trademark Office by Biblica, Inc.™

Scripture taken from the New King James Version®. Copyright © 1982 by Thomas Nelson. Used by permission. All rights reserved.

Scripture quotations marked (NLT) are taken from the *Holy Bible, New Living Translation*, copyright © 1996, 2004, 2007, 2013 by Tyndale House Foundation. Used by permission of Tyndale House Publishers, Inc., Carol Stream, Illinois 60188. All rights reserved.

Scripture taken from the New Century Version®. Copyright © 2005 by Thomas Nelson. Used by permission. All rights reserved.

Scripture quotations taken from the New American Standard Bible®, Copyright © 1960, 1962, 1963, 1968, 1971, 1972, 1973, 1975, 1977, 1995 by the Lockman Foundation. Used by permission

Scripture quotations from *The Message*. Copyright © by Eugene H. Peterson 1993, 1994, 1995, 1996, 2000, 2001, 2002. Used by permission of Tyndale House Publishers, Inc.

All other copyrighted material contained herein referenced at source.

The views expressed here-in remain the sole responsibility of the authors, who exempt the publisher from all liability. The authors and publisher do not assume responsibility for any loss, damage, or disruption caused by the contents, errors or omissions, whether such contents, errors or omissions result from opinion, negligence, accident, or any other cause, and hereby disclaim any and all liability to any party.

ISBN: 978-0-6484602-3-7

For Jesus,
the author and finisher of our faith (Hebrews chapter 12 verse 2)
and to the next generation of writers.

CONTENTS

Foreword ix

Section 1
Regeneration 1

Embrace the new!—Elise Pappas	3
Positioned with a purpose—Araina Kazia Pereira	7
Freedom from fear—Jo Fuller	11
An Identity Crisis—Jessica Knell	15
I am Jonah—Petro Swart	19
Time to Ponder—Joseph F. Kolapudi	23
Blue or Red—Neville Hiatt	27
From dust to gold—Amy Manners	31
I am because You are—Araina Kazia Pereira	35
The armour of God: gospel of peace—Nic Lee	39

Section 2
Breaking through 45

Road to Damascus—Amy Manners	47
What would Russell do?—Russell Modlin	51
Being in the middle—Esther Koh	55
Lost my way—Joseph Kolapudi	59
Here and Now in the interlude—Araina Kazia Pereira	63
Get out of your own way—Jesse Moore	67
A young horse is no good until he's started —John Skinner	69
Convenient cross—Petro Swart	73
Singing through the shadows—Rebecca Howan	77
Prayer, the most intimate conversation—Kevin Park	81
Finding freedom—Matthew Thornton	85
You run with horses now—Amy Manners	89

Section 3
Family, friends and the body of Christ   93

Good friends are good for the soul—Rebecca Howan	95
Train Brakes—John Skinner	99
Religion verses Relationship—Jo Fuller	103
How God turned my loneliness into a blessing—Jessica McPherson	107
Everyone has a superpower—Kristen Dang	111
Jane Eyre and the question: is there such a thing as 'the one'?—Rebecca Moore	115
The uncertainties of a new year—Esther Koh	119
Involuntary celibacy in the digital church—Blake Gardiner	123
Jesus knows how this feels—Cartia Moore	127
Granny get your gun—John Skinner	131
Drama! Who needs it?—Rebecca Moore	135
A faith boost—Manuele Teofilo	139
A duty of care—Jessica Knell	143

Section 4
Culturality   147

Redeeming culture—Jesse Moore	149
A political or apolitical God?—Roydon Ng	153
Jesus didn't tap out—Jeremy Dover	157
Love, more than a feeling—Matthew Thornton	161
Trust the process—Elise Pappas	165
Should I give up being a Dad?—Russell Modlin	169
In the middle?—David Goodwin	175
Who is the antichrist?—Jeremy Dover	179
Supermorality—David Goodwin	183
How should a Christian vote?—Roydon Ng	187
The armour of God: belt of truth—Nic Lee	191

Section 5
Visions and Dreams 195

God, the storywriter—Kevin Park	197
A beautiful reminder—Elise Pappas	201
Are you brave again?—Cartia Moore	205
A drawer called oblivion—Travis Barnes	209
Inspired by a step of faith—Joseph F. Kolapudi	213
Step into the light—Kristen Dang	217
Serving from a wheelchair—Manuele Teofilo	221
If you're not comforted by Revelation, you're reading it wrong—Jessica McPherson	225

Section 6
Intentionality 229

The me I used to be —Travis Barnes	231
Your calling does not save you —Blake Gardiner	235
Why a loving God can't just let everyone into heaven —Jessica McPherson	239
Becoming deliberate —Rebecca Moore	243
Go and see the stars —Matthew Thornton	247
Words, and hearing the voice of God —Cartia Moore	251
The gateway to worship —Jessica Knell	255
Hit snooze and choose joy—Petro Swart	259
Dear child of God —Jo Fuller	263
The armour of God: helmet of salvation —Nic Lee	267
The perfect workout —Jesse Moore	271

About the authors 277

Foreword

Question—having been the Australian cricket team chaplain for 17 years to 2000, then sideways to Life After Cricket since 2001, written 24 books, and Christian articles regularly published around the world through the Ramon Williams Religious Media unit, with Delma my wife of 43 years, four adult children and now grand parents, what other solemn challenge was on the horizon?

Strangely, the Lord had 'prepared the way' for a new faith adventure (we have been faith financed since 1977). In 2005 I established 'Press Service International' to promote my Christian articles around the world, as the remarkable elderly Ramon Williams indicated he was to shortly curtail his media enterprise.

In 2008 Christian Today Australia (on-line) editor Szeleng Chan rang me inviting me to write a daily article. A year later, a new editor, David Chang, met me over coffee and suggested adding a daily sport article. That was too much, yet David Chang warmed to my idea of having five young people write a sport article for each week day.

A year later, having seen this young sport writers boom, the young writer ministry expanded to include other young people and a broad range of topics. Today, 10 years later, with the gracious support of Mr Basil Sellers AM, there are 105 young writers aged between 18-30 years from Australia, New Zealand, and around the world.

This has now been acknowledged at the highest level. 'Press Service International' was awarded the Australasian

Religious Press Association (ARPA) 2019 premier award, 'The Gutenberg'. This young writer ministry was celebrated by Australia and New Zealand's major Christian media with their peer annual top award.

With Rebecca Moore, one of our editors and senior writers, having written two highly successful books and, with her husband Tony, developed a book publishing arm, along came the idea for an anthology of young writer articles. I stand in awe of the fact that the Lord had 'prepared the way' as promised in the Book of Jonah—the text I addressed at the 2019 young writers conference in Melbourne.

Dr Mark Tronson

Section one

REGENERATION

EMBRACE THE NEW!

by Elise Pappas

Recently I was standing at the beach, right on the shoreline. It was a beautiful but cloudy day, the seas were rough and I stood there watching the waves as they rolled in and crashed right near me. There were rips and the waves rolled in inconsistently. Even though there seemed to be so much uncertainty with it all, the one thing that was consistent was the knowledge that the tide was coming in and that, in due time, it would go back out again.

It made me think about life and how at different points some things can seem a bit rough and rocky, uncertain, even not fair. Regardless, however things seem, the one thing that remains constant through it all is our Heavenly Father.

Seasons are a part of life, that's how God created the Earth. It says in the book of Genesis, chapter one, verse 14, on the fourth day of creation God said:

> "Let there be lights in the expanse of the heavens to separate the day from the night. And let them be for signs and for seasons, and for days and years". (ESV)

Shifting seasons

Things shift, things change. Nothing really ever remains exactly the same and thank goodness for this! How monotonous would life be if they did?

The one thing that I am grateful for is that regardless of how things may seem, His plans and purposes for us do not change—He is constant. In the Book of Numbers chapter 23, verse 19 it says:

> God is not human, that he should lie, not a human being, that he should change his mind. Does he speak and then not act? Does he promise and not fulfil? (NIV)

If He has purposed it, it will happen. It's inevitable that our job title or job description will change, our pay package may differ, our expectations for our own life might not always reflect our current reality, and friendships may change. However, the one thing that does not change is who He has called me to be—first and foremostly a woman (or man) of God.

Constant God

When we understand this we realise that everything else is peripheral. Even if something changes in my life it doesn't change who He has called me to be. If for a season I do something different—like become a full-time mother, or be off work or out of action for a season due to health issues—it doesn't change who I am in God, or mean that this season is any less significant than the last. Truth be told, I believe every new unfolding chapter or season will be our most significant one to date!

The interesting thing I have found is that when we become content and secure in this, and as we surround ourselves with good people, we come to learn that when things change, it actually brings greater clarity and focus regarding the plans that God has for us.

It also helps us to understand the significance of the place in which we find ourselves, so rather than wishing we were still in the last season—still at the last job, still in the last relationship, or still on that last overseas holiday—we can freely embrace the new season that He has set before us.

So, how should we respond to a change in season? Understand the season you find yourself in—enjoy it, make the most of it, find new and greater purpose in it, and believe that season is significant—then it will be your greatest one yet!

POSITIONED WITH A PURPOSE

by Araina Kazia Pereira

The age old question: why does God who is all-knowing and loving let bad things happen to good people? Whilst it's hard to give a concrete answer to that, there are a few things that we should know about good, evil and our circumstances.

We ask questions like: Why does God allow cancer? Broken families? Terrorism or abuse? Or why does God allow mass murder? Yet we often forget that the same God that we accuse of allowing bad things to occur let the worst thing possible happen to his son. We often ask why if God loves us why does he let bad things happen to us; yet we forget that He loved His only begotten son—yet let him suffer. Why?

There was a purpose for this suffering and there was a purpose in the position that He placed Jesus in (Acts 2:22-24). Often it can be the same for us—even though we may not like it, God is intentional and purposeful, even in suffering. Suffering can come in many forms and for various reasons. It can come in the form of punishment (Judges 2:11-15). It can provoke repentance (Psalm 119:71).

It can be used to grow God's kingdom (1 Peter 4:12-19), but also to bring justice (Romans 9:19-26). It is important to note that not all bad things come from God—in fact evil in its purest form comes from the devil, and sometimes suffering is inflicted in this way (Job 1-2).

You can love God, but struggle to understand why He is letting you suffer when you have been devoted to walking in His ways. Habbakuk was the same. He thought he knew God, and he loved God, but he wrestled with suffering and why God was allowing it (Habakkuk 1:2-4). It is important to remember that while God is loving and compassionate, He is also fair and just. Like a good father, He will discipline His children. However, suffering is not always punishment from God, nor is it always a test of faith. Yet, we automatically look to God when we suffer.

So how can we respond when we suffer?

A posture of faith

As hard as it is, bad times call for a posture of faith, not one of contempt. So often we can go to God in frustration and anguish that he is letting us suffer when we have been faithful. Yet we forget that God has always been faithful and even in the suffering he will continue to be faithful.

A posture of faith calls us to identify and respond to the promise within suffering. Everything that God does he does with thought and, if the suffering is coming from the enemy, then God will bring justice to the unjust (Numbers 10:9). However, it will be done in His timing and in His way (Jeremiah 1:19).

A posture of faith will look like a steering away from comparison. Don't compare the rate of your healing to someone else's healing, or the timing of someone else's breakthrough with the way you are waiting for your own breakthrough. Comparison leads to complacency of faith, not a posture of faith. A posture of faith starts with prayer, whether in your own suffering or someone else's.

Respond by identifying and seeking the promise and purpose that is to come from the suffering. God's timing and will is certain, what is in His timing will come to pass and what isn't...won't. Activated faith looks like obedience and praise. Both Habbakah (3:16-18) and Joshua (6:6-20) understood this. Even in their time of trial they obeyed the Lord and they praised Him for this works, proclaiming their faith. They knew that even in the midst of their battle that God had the upper hand, and had equipped them to win.

A posture of faith looks like finding a blessing in all seasons—even the hard ones. In our trials, choosing to find blessing in the ability to bless others through testimony, learn from mistakes, and praise God through obedience. In our wins, choosing to praise God for them and asking Him to reveal how to use them to proclaim His glory.

In both instances, the trials and the wins, it's about realising the position you are in can be used to bless others and brings others—as well as yourself—closer in relationship to God. Whether that be through repentance, testimonies, prayer—the list goes on—it's about finding the purpose in the position and knowing that God's timing and plan is good, and will see you win.

God is faithful, and intentional, always. Even in suffering He has positioned us for victory.

FREEDOM FROM FEAR

by Jo Fuller

Fear in all its ugly forms, wants to wrap itself around us in a thick, dark blanket.

Keeping us in hiding; stuck, frozen, trapped.

Like a web, it spins its many lies. Sometimes subtle, sometimes not.

The hidden cause of many ailments, sickness and pain, can be traced back to this twisted, rotten root.

It never wants to un-grip its tight hold; it is the opposite of love, therefore its result can only mean destruction.

Disguised in many ways; some may not realise its seeped into the depths of their soul.

But I want out, to break free. Not just for a while, a nice reprieve.

No! I want to be forever free from its hold, so I can step into all He has for me.

Freedom

What does it mean to be truly free? Free from the oppressive nature of fear.

I don't want it to be a nice notion, or an emotional song to be sung. We may know the right words to say, religious banter to appear pious.

But what if we were actually, truly free?

Free from the chains that bind us. That suppress us, oppress us, that hold us back, and keep us muted.

Free from the stuff that stops us from being fully alive in Him.

That stops us from living in the light as true sons and daughters of Christ. To be SET free; unchained, unbound, unleashed. Free to release all that we have in Him.

This is the life Christ promises us, this is the life he wants for us, this is the New Life spoken of in Colossians, chapter three.

The battle rages

And so, the battle rages…

Standing from a place of victory reassures me I have already won, and yet the battle ensues and at times I take a hit.

But with each inch moved forward, I know I am taking ground.

Knowing who I am in Christ and who resides within,
helps me to stand strong and distinguish a lie masquerading as truth.

We have been given a complete set of armour to protect us as we fight against the accuser.

Lord, help me to remember to put on truth as my belt, faith as my shield and salvation as my helmet (Ephesians chapter six, verses 10-18).

2 Timothy chapter one, verse seven, says, 'We have not been given a spirit of fear, but the Holy Spirit gives us mighty power, love and a sound mind'.

May these truths become my reality, one thought at a time.

Perfect love casts out fear

So, what can cast away fear?
Lord, you say it is Love. Perfect love expels all fear (1 John chapter four, verse 18).

When I think of Perfect Love, Lord it is you. Giving us your son, Christ Jesus, so we can come boldly to you and experience this Love.

May our love for you become greater than our love for anything or anyone else.

May our reverential fear of you Lord, take away our fear of man.

Help us to continually set our minds on things above and to cast our cares and worries on you.

Help us come like little children and find shelter under your wings.

Let perfect love manifest within so our love can grow more

perfect. For you and for others.

Help us experience this perfect love; the love that expels all fear. (1 John chapter four, verses 17-19)

AN IDENTITY CRISIS
by Jessica Knell

Identity. It shapes who we believe we are and how we choose to interact with the world around us.

Amidst our current mental health crisis, it is imperative that young people today are supported to discover their true identity. Furthermore, the popularity boom of self-help books, podcasts and TedTalks reflect society's widespread yearning for discovering the source of secure identity.

Through a vicious cycle of hyper-examination, we seek to reveal our true selves by staring deeper and deeper into our internal mirror. We sing along with the secular chorus, chanting that our identity is found within ourselves.

However, the danger is, that we alone are empty vessels. The internal pursuit for identity is void unless we have an external reference frame from which to view ourselves. As Christians our reference frame is Christ.

Answering the Big Questions

> For you created my inmost being; you knit me together in my mother's womb. I praise you because I am fearfully and wonderfully made; your works are wonderful, I know that full well. (Psalm 139, verses 13-14 NIV)

Who am I and what is my purpose?

Perhaps one of the greatest human struggles is our attempt to answer the above questions. Universally we each strive to understand who we are and what our purpose is.

Some may seek solace in relationships, occupation or personal achievements however, this is fleeting. When a transient basis for identity fails us, we vainly rummage to pick up the pieces to make ourselves whole.

The millennia saw the continued rise of individualism and the advent of the 'snowflake' generation. Our secular society sells identity seekers psychological tests or new-age therapies designed to deepen the individuals' awareness of themselves.

Although, psychological knowledge can function as guide to understanding ones-self, in isolation of Christ it is redundant in understanding true identity.

Our lives are a wonderfully messy tapestry of earthly disappointments, grace and God's abundant love. Undervaluing our identity negates our inherent worth as children knitted together in our mother's womb by the Creator of the Universe.

Answering the Ultimate Question

> "I am the Alpha and the Omega," says the Lord God, "who is, and who was, and who is to come, the Almighty." (Revelation chapter 1, verse 8 NIV)

The ultimate question—the answer to life, the universe and everything in between:

Who is God?

In Isaiah chapter 64, verse 8, it is written that we are the clay and God is the potter—we are all the work of His hand. This poetic metaphor depicts an artist lovingly moulding His beautiful masterpiece. We are the clay.

Additionally, Matthew chapter 10, verses 29-31, continues to echo God's intimate love for His creation. If the Creator of the Universe cares for every individual sparrow, imagine how much more He cares for us—worth more than many sparrows.

The biblical narrative shares the greatest love story ever written. Whereby, God sacrifices His only Son for the redemption of humanity. In its entirety, the Bible reveals the character of God. He is the Alpha and Omega, the Lamb and the great 'I am'.

Therefore, with all things considered, it can be concluded our true source of identity may only be understood once we begin to understand the character of God.

Freedom in Identity

> For we are God's handiwork, created in Christ Jesus to do good works, which God prepared in advance for us to do. (Ephesians chapter 2, verse 10 NIV)

If people understood their true identity secured in Christ, it would radically change the world. Not only would individuals internally comprehend their value, they would also understand the inherent worth contained within one another.

No longer would selfish indulgence and the pleasure of self be considered desirable. Instead, we would seek to love our God above all else and love others as ourselves.

Imagine the culture change if we, as Christians, strove to not only understand the source of our true identity but also the identity of one another.

I AM JONAH

by Petro Swart

Is it a push or a pull? One of the biggest questions I have ever been asked.

The last five years have been marked by constant transitions for me: between countries; between cities; between houses; between jobs. When discussing my latest grand plan for adventure, a wise friend asked me, "Petro, are you leaving because of a push or a pull?"

In response to my quiet confusion he explained further, was I drawn to leave because I was trying to escape something here or because I was chasing something there? I felt obliged to say a pull, because running away is wrong is it not? Guilt encapsulated me upon answering though, because I had been Jonah-ing and was not quite ready to give up that comfort yet.

Here I sat, contently in the belly of a big fish. I was indeed running away from my Nineveh. The difference between Jonah and I was that I had my eyes squeezed shut with all my might—determined to ignore the stench of kelp and the slime knotting in my hair. Denial sat between me and being spat out on a beach.

The issue with trying to follow in the footsteps of Jonah, is that I seemed to have forgotten how the story ended. Eventually the smell and ick got the better of me and I succumbed to the admitting that I was indeed running away.

God's grace vs. Our justice

Like Jonah, I knew that my God is a faithful God. I knew that when I called out, my Father would rescue me. I just pictured it differently from how it actually happened.

I pictured the fish disintegrating into thin air, a five-star shower and fresh outfit appearing on the beach, and then going back to the comfort of my own home. Someone else could go to Nineveh. God would show me complete, undeserved grace.

God's grace instead looked like being vomited up on a beach and realising my fate—I was going to Nineveh anyway. This time though, I got to go covered in fish-muck. Safe from a storm, but still a bit worse for wear.

My ego a little bruised, but thankful to be on dry land again, I expected God's grace to look the same for the situation I was returning to as it did for me. Surprise, surprise, though, putting God in a box does not work. He is bigger than my expectations and His grace is not dependent on my sense of justice.

Long story short, it did not happen. The people I wanted to be walloped with the full wrath of God were showered with gifts, while my life just seemed to be getting tougher.

Jonah's (my) response

> But to Jonah this seemed very wrong, and he became angry. He prayed to the Lord, "Isn't this what I said, Lord, when I was still at home? That is what I tried to forestall by fleeing to Tarshish. I knew that you are a gracious and compassionate God, slow to anger and abounding in love,

a God who relents from sending calamity. Now, Lord, take away my life, for it is better for me to die than to live."

But the Lord replied, "Is it right for you to be angry?" (Jonah chapter 4, verses 1 to 4 NIV)

I felt entitled to my anger; at the 'injustice' of God. As if I could tell God how this story was supposed to end, and how His grace should be defined.

Even when God tried to graciously show me that He was working on a bigger plan, and while my story was part of others' it was not comparable. I could not compare my successes and/or failures to those of the people around me. I was in my own season learning different lessons.

I returned to Nineveh in order to be able to leave because of a pull rather than a push. In the midst of my frustration with how unfair God's grace was, I was still desperate to leave my situation. I was still leaving because of a push.

Is a pull better?

As it turns out, the healthier option hurts. A lot. Leaving a situation because of the pull of another means that you are comfortable in your current place. The absence of a push results in a heavier launch—it's harder to pull something than it is to push it. There is a certain resistance to leaving.

If the new situation was not there, would leaving be attractive? What if the new situation is not all that glamourous? Entering into a new season, or being obedient to God's prompting, with the right heart-attitude is still uncomfortable.

If Jonah had just left for Nineveh with the intent to obey God and play his humble part in saving the city, how would the story have been different? What if the story of Jonah is not in the Bible to show us God's grace in saving Nineveh, but rather the gentle patience with which He taught Jonah?

This piece is somewhat unfinished, because I have not leapt yet, and still wrestle with whether leaving for a pull is working for me. I know though, that my God is faithful, gracious and steadfast. He would not have called me to Nineveh for both me and the city to go up in flames. Both Jonah and Nineveh 'won' in the end—it just took Jonah longer to get to his victory because God needed to fix his heart first.

Maybe after this adventure I can write a sequel to Jonah's story: Nineveh revisited (without the fish this time)? Here's hoping anyway…

TIME TO PONDER
by Joseph F. Kolapudi

When was the last time you just sat there and did nothing? It seems like a silly question, but humour me. Simply taking the time to be 'in the moment' may not be a waste of time—it might be the antidote to a life that seems to perpetually be in motion. The moments that seem insignificant can actually prove, in time, to be the most important.

I recently returned from a trip to Germany where I was attending a work conference, and towards the end of my time there, I was quite exhausted. I hadn't really taken the time to take everything in, and it was actually weighing me down—to the point where I felt physically ill.

A breath of fresh air

There was a particular moment where I actually felt...well... helpless. I was alone at a table drinking tea when someone I didn't know struck up a conversation. It was a breath of fresh air, and I relished it. But, what I didn't know was that the conversation I was about to have was to have a deeper impact than I actually realised.

I had only two days earlier realised that the place where I was staying would not be able to accommodate me for the remainder of my stay, and a friend who I thought I would be able to stay with was travelling out of the country. I didn't know anyone else I could stay with; that is, until I met this stranger at the conference.

Without even mentioning the need for a place to stay, the stranger pulled out the address of where he was staying and said if I ever needed a place to stay, he had a guest house close to his office where visitors often could be accommodated at no charge.

I was flabbergasted. How could he possibly know that I needed a place to stay? Was he just being nice? Could this really be true? I hesitated. Perhaps it would be too much to ask.

Battle of the soul

Sometimes, in moments like these, we find ourselves caught between what I like to call a battle of the soul. Our minds often think in hypotheticals—what can happen, and what should occur. However, when it comes to the soul, we usually act on what our hearts convict us of. It is not a matter of wit or will, but rather, a pondering of what is possible.

I ended up catching up to my newfound friend and asking him if I could, in fact, take him up on his offer. He willingly obliged, and a phone call later, I found myself with a train ticket in hand and a place to stay for the next forty-eight hours. My friend entertained me for the next few days, accompanied me on my journey, hosted me at his house for meals, and even paid for my travels. It was truly a blessing in disguise, and one that I could have taken for granted if my head had overruled my heart.

Reflecting on purpose

So, on the train journey to my final destination, when my

newfound friend had faded into the distance on the train platform and I finally found myself alone once again, I took the time to ponder.

Life certainly has a way of teaching us lessons we would otherwise try to avoid. Trusting a stranger takes a lot of courage but blessing a stranger who perhaps cannot return the favour takes even more. For my newfound friend, it was worth the time.

Finding purpose in moments of life that seem beyond our control can take time to understand. But in the end, we are all the better for it; because in those moments where our future seems so unclear, we find a God to whom we can entrust both our deepest fears, and our most fearless longings. We then realise what it takes to make time, instead of admitting we don't have any.

I wonder if we take the time to ponder, life's purpose might become a little clearer.

BLUE OR RED?
by Neville Hiatt

You take the blue pill—the story ends, you wake up in your bed and believe whatever you want to believe. You take the red pill—you stay in Wonderland, and I show you how deep the rabbit hole goes. Remember: all I'm offering is the truth. Nothing more. (The Matrix)

They grew up in a world that conditioned them to take the blue pill without even thinking. It would be decades before they would reunite and realise just how foolish they had been.

She thought he was too good for her. So, not only did she do nothing, but she suffered in silence whenever her friend talked about him. Her friend also liked him.

He thought of her as a friend and had no idea she liked him. He was smitten by her friend, though, but like her thought she was too good for him, and thus took no action.

Where do we get this belief from that someone is too good for us or they are out of our league? Sadly, I've heard it said just as much in churches as I have in school playgrounds.

It would be years later that he would find out his friend had been heartbroken when he came back to school after the holidays in a new relationship. It would be another decade before he found out she had liked him too.

All three people from very different backgrounds, different countries, different cultures, different beliefs, yet all intersecting at this one point in time. All three conditioned to believe that they were less than they were created to be. All three making choices based on their feelings which would have life long consequences.

Both girls grew to be women, got married, and are now mothers. How differently their lives could have turned out if their identity more closely resembled who they were created to be. The rest of their story is theirs to tell, and to impart what they have learned on the next generation. The only story I can delve into any real depth on is his...because it is mine. I have no prodigy so I leave my thoughts here for you to dissect.

Did you grow up believing similar things?
Do you still hear it in your community now?
How different could the next decade be if we all started taking the red pill?
How long would it take for the ripple effect to circumnavigate the globe?

Even if you are the only person to read this don't underestimate the impact you could have. Every hero and every villain throughout history were all just individuals. The only difference is the force that they let govern their life and the identity this gave them.

It's amazing to now see in Melbourne that one of the main sports and entertainment arenas is sponsored by Marvel. A single franchise, albeit a hugely successful one, has made and expects to continue to make enough money to perceive becoming the naming rights sponsor of an arena as a profitable advertising expense.

Looking back on my own childhood, I remember not even thinking twice about Lois Lane being unable to work out that Clark Kent was also Superman. Now; it's like it's only a pair of glasses—how could everyone not guess his secret identity?

Yet, how many comics would they have sold if every character in the story possessed the confidence of Superman? How many movies and TV episodes would have made it to our screens if Clark acted the same in both roles?

Who we believe we are affects everything we think, say, and do. I wouldn't have written any blog posts when I was in school, not only was blogging not a thing, I would have been too self-conscious. But, now I can tell either of those friends my true thoughts and feelings because my identity isn't dependent on their reply.

Living a fearless life is so liberating—it's like I'm living life looking like Clark Kent yet feeling and thinking as boldly as Superman, and as fearlessly. There is no kryptonite in my life, I don't even fear death, it's only the loss of temporal time. How dramatically one's life can change from only a few years ago when I was scared of non-existent things coming out from behind every tree and driveway I went past.

Our minds are a very powerful tool and we have the power to govern their output.

So I ask you, what is your choice—the blue pill or the red pill?

> But I need to love you Lord more than my Life. But to die to myself isn't easy.
> (Choose You This Day – Harvest Band)

FROM DUST TO GOLD

by Amy Manners

> Down below, the earth is melted by fire.
> Here the rocks contain precious lapis lazuli,
> And the dust contains gold...
> Uncover the precious stones...
> Bring to light the hidden treasures.
> (Job chapter 28, verses 5-11 NLT)

In your deep places, where your world is melted by fire; wedged into the rock of hard circumstances and hidden below the surface of what others see—yes, even in your darkness—lies all that is precious to God.

The gold He is melting and moulding and reshaping in your heart isn't found in the palaces of your achievements, but in the dust of humility. To be broken, crushed, and crumbled so the only jewel that remains is Christ: this is our holy pursuit.

I once heard a whisper, "Many strive to go higher, but it's wiser to go lower. Many seek to scale the heights, but it's more valuable to search the depths".

As I mined through the hard stone and dug through the darkness, I discovered the greatest treasure: Calvary's Cross. Christ was crucified in the darkness, Christ was buried in the rock of hard places, Christ was crushed to secure our salvation.

> He was pierced for our transgressions,
> he was crushed for our iniquities;
> the punishment that brought us peace was on him,
> and by his wounds we are healed.
> (Isaiah chapter 53, verses 4-5 NIV)

Wounds that heal

We are accustomed to seek out those who appear strong to bring healing and support—yet in the depths I found One with wounds that heal. Only Christ knows the depths of our suffering because He alone has carried our brokenness. He hung with strength that looked like weakness: a whip-slashed back, nail-pierced hands and feet, breaths seared with exhaustion, and a heart that failed, broken by the weight of crucifixion.

> He heals the brokenhearted
> And binds up their wounds.
> (Psalm chapter 147, verse 3 NIV)

He can heal your broken heart because His heart was broken for the love of you. He can bind up your wounds because He was wounded for the joy set before Him: an eternity with you.

Love's victory

Because of all Christ endured, you can feel safe inviting His Spirit to search the dusty tunnels of your heart. You can trust Him for He will retrieve gold from dust and diamonds from rock.

Love's victory pushed aside the stone of a defeated grave—and in that moment all your treasures hidden in darkness met the light of the risen Christ. There are jewels that can only be forged in hard places, these treasures your King will wear in His crown for all to see, for this is His testimony of the overcoming power at work in your life. When all you see is dust, He sees specks of gold, and brings them out of hiding.

In your deep places, where your world is melted by fire, wedged into the rock of hard circumstances and hidden below the surface of what others see—yes even in your darkness—is a secret place where deep calls to deep, where wounded hands uphold you with an everlasting love, and where a holy heart that was broken makes yours forever whole.

I AM BECAUSE YOU ARE...

by Araina Kazia Pereira

"Who is God?" and "Who am I?" are two questions that we often ask in isolation of each other. Yet, the answers to both those questions are interlaced, provoking us, for in order to understand one we must try to uncover the other.

For most of our journey we are trying to answer those two fundamental questions. As humans, the concept of identity is constantly evolving, changing, growing as we grow, and shaped by our experiences, surroundings, beliefs, values and those around us. In pursuit of our identity we can so often fall into the trap of pursuing the world, its labels, statuses, and perception.

We can turn to the world to define us. However; we are created in and through Christ. Our identity is derived from who God is, and who He has called us to be. Yet so often, we forget to listen to what He has already said, and has set in stone about who we are created to be.

I am...

Biblically God has given new names to many, renaming them to signify the calling that they have. Abram became Abraham, Sarai became Sarah, Jacob became Israel, and Simon became Peter. These names resembled prophecy, promise, and the calling on these lives.

While the Bible doesn't give us new names as such, it does help us to uncover our identity as desired and planned by God. We can come to understand that we are all children of God (John 1:12), created by Him for a purpose (Ephesians 2:10); and an heir of Christ (Romans 8:2).

While these terms are a lot harder to understand compared to societal labels; the way in which God identifies his people throughout Scripture brings light to what we are commissioned to do, affirms the significance of Christ (1 Corinthians 6:11), and gives us hope for the future. It gives us a purpose (Matthew 5:14), and equips us to fulfil it (2 Corinthians 4:16).

In the grand scheme of things, this gives us eternal identity—not the superficial identity that the world labels us with. And, through trying to uncover who God is, this eternal identity is revealed to us. Why do we have to look to who God is? We are His handiwork (Ephesians 2:10), created by Him.

Just as we are identified by name from our parents, so we are also identified by God through His word. And through uncovering who He is we can understand what it means to be identified as a child of God, what responsibility it holds, and the part we play in His family.

But where do you even go in order to begin to understand who God is when you can't see him?

…because you are…

One of the most powerful verses in the Bible comes from Exodus chapter 3 verses 13-15 where God identifies himself to Moses. 'I am who I am'. It's no coincidence that the Hebrew translation 'e'heyeh' is related to the most common identification of God, 'YHWH'—identifying Yahweh in terms of the original 'I am' statement given to Moses. While we will never fully understand God or His nature, this statement begins to set the story for who God is. In its simplest form; God affirmed His existence to Moses, his unchanging yet inexhaustible nature.

These 'I am' statements are then replicated and affirmed in the flesh seven times by Jesus in the New Testament: I am the bread of life (John 6:35); I am the light of the world (John 8:12); I am the door (John 10:9); I am the good shepherd (John 10:11); I am the resurrection and the life (John 11:25-26); I am the way, the truth and the life (John 14:6); I am the vine (John 15:5).

He is everything that humanity needed in order for it to be possible for us to be in relationship with God. Drawing us a connection to our identity as designed by God, through the purpose of the cross.

The central part of this story shines light on the answer to both those questions. The cross became a bridge that connects us to God. It changes who we are, taking us from who we were to who God has called and designed us to be. It is a bridge, set on the strong foundation, not a see-saw for us to go back and forth on. As with most things with God, it was certain and intentional.

Being a part of the body of Christ means that in order to understand who we are we must first seek out who God is— and through that He reveals our identity and His plans for us. The word identity itself has two meanings: 'the fact of being who or what a person is' and 'a close similarity or affinity.' By virtue of this, it's evident we must seek to uncover who God is first, because we indeed have been created in His likeness and image (Genesis 1:27).

…God.

THE ARMOUR OF GOD: GOSPEL OF PEACE

by Nic Lee

Stand firm then, with the belt of truth buckled around your waist, with the breastplate of righteousness in place, and with your feet fitted with the readiness that comes from the gospel of peace. (Ephesians chapter 6, verses 14 – 15 NIV)

Good news in the form of a Saviour is the main message of the Bible, particularly the New Testament. Jesus taught that the good news was that the Kingdom of God was near at hand. His life, death and resurrection as the gateway to the Kingdom of God is thus the ultimate gospel– the Gospel. Paul wrote of the gospel describing it as good news that both was peaceful and would bring about peace.

The Kingdom of God is about reconciliation and being at peace with God. Jesus also taught the disciples not just about the Gospel itself, but also how to approach delivering it to the various towns and places throughout the region of Galilee.

The key characteristic to describe the Gospel is 'peace'. This stands in stark contrast to the various ideas that were already in the mindset of the general public. The Jews generally were well-versed with the prophecies that they would receive a deliverer and Saviour.

Unfortunately, their worldly mindset meant their idea of a

Messiah would be a political leader who would physically restore the nation and free them from the oppression of Roman authority. Jesus was clear that his message, and the Kingdom, was built on a foundation of love and peace, not violence or the sword.

Peace is not just a description of the nature of the Gospel, or its delivery—we will achieve peace and reconciliation with God. In Ephesians chapter 2, verse 14, Paul describes Jesus as 'our peace, who has made us both one and has broken down the dividing wall of hostility'. In verse 17, Jesus 'came and preached peace to you who were far off and peace to those who were near for through him we have access in one Spirit to the Father'.

Application and Testimony

The analogous item in the armoury for the Gospel are sandals. We are to wear the Gospel to protect our feet. As part of our morning routine, and before we leave home, we can be reminded that as we put our shoes on, we are also arming ourselves with the Gospel. As we look ahead to each day, we can be reminded that God has provided us with the entire armour, and as we wear our shoes, we have His protection to keep us safe from being tempted and falling into sin.

We may have oversimplified the understanding of the Gospel that we are to wear, but a proper contextualisation and interpretation helps us to appreciate it is more a readiness of the gospel of peace that we are to have on our feet. Think of it as being ready to move about with the Gospel.

Having a gospel of peace mindset allows us to be agile and adaptable to the various situations we find ourselves in. If we are connected into the headship of God, He may direct us in the way we represent Jesus to the people around us. Sometimes, when you bump into people on your daily commute into work, God will create opportunities for you to share His goodness and Gospel with them.

Sometimes, it is not a direct 'this is the Gospel message' either. You can infuse the Gospel truths into the way you talk, and also in between everything that you share, and thus provide God's love in a holistic package. Sometimes, loving other people means just listening in a non-judgemental way, so that you build trust with them.

Prayer

Dear God,

I thank you for providing us with your Gospel. I thank you for making the message so meaningful and adaptable to the everyday situations of my own life, and I'm sure, for everyone else. No matter what our culture and background, You and Your Gospel bring us peace.

As I get up each morning, invariably to go to work, I thank You for the provision that I have plenty of choice in what I wear. Help me to actively choose You and Your Gospel to be part of the overall armour You equip us with.

As I walk these steps of life, literally, to the car, to the train and the office, may you guide my steps that I may walk beside you and in pathways of Your wisdom, truth, love and peace. Help me to see the people around me through Your loving eyes, so that I may represent You well to them, in minor little ways.

Make fragrant and permeate my conversations with people,

both believers and non-believers, with your Gospel truth and peaceful nature, so that they are encouraged and blessed. Help me continue to be a peacemaker, finding solutions or just being a friendly and supportive presence in the journeys which are more difficult to bear.

For those who are made weary and heavy-hearted by the situations of life and hopeless circumstances, help me to intercede for them, such that their burdens can be placed at the foot of Your cross. Where society breaks down, where norms of law and order are challenged, help people to see You.

Though the darkness of the world grows evermore, remind us that Your light shines ever brighter in contrast. Your Gospel is peace. Your presence within the believer is an unwavering source of warmth, energy and hope for a world which fights with itself, and with You.

As our Heavenly gardener, rain down Your living streams of water so that we Your people will drink and not thirst. Prune the weeds and show us the fertile friendly soil of individuals who are eager and ready to receive the blessing that is Your Gospel truth. Where there are concrete-type environments, and the Gospel message is rejected, help us to dust our feet off and move onto greener pastures.

May Your peace be with us.
In Jesus Name.
Amen.

> When peace like a river, attends my way,
> When sorrows like sea billows roll
> Whatever my lot, You have taught me to say
> It is well, it is well, with my soul

GOD IN LIFE

(It is Well with My Soul, Philip Paul Bless and
Christopher Stafford)

Section Two

Breaking Through

ROAD TO DAMASCUS

by Amy Manners

On the road to Damascus, surrounded by mountains, lies a village soaked in cool air and dappled sunlight. Here, birds sing from olive trees that cast soft shadows over the courtyards of ancient monasteries.

Legend has it that Saint Tekla, the daughter of a pagan prince and disciple of Saint Paul, fled to these rugged mountains in the first century to escape persecution. Those who threatened to kill her were in hot pursuit of her life, but her way was blocked by jagged rock. So, she fell to her knees, and cried to God.

The tale goes that in response God parted the mountains for Tekla so she could hide in one of the many caves. To this day the place where she took refuge is called Ma'loula, which in Aramaic means 'entrance'.

Even though this story enters the realm of myth, the caves of Ma'loula have provided cover for persecuted Christians throughout the centuries. The village is home to one of the oldest Christian communities in the world. Nuns live side by side with their Muslim neighbours in peaceful tolerance.

Ma'loula is one of only three villages where Aramaic—the pre-Islamic language of Syria—is still spoken. Aramaic was the language of Jesus.

When the war began

The inhabitants of Ma'loula wanted nothing to do with the Syrian civil war that raged around them. But even this oasis of peace was not exempt from the chaos. In September 2013, a Jordanian suicide bomber blew up a truck at the village's entrance, killing eight people. Two months later 12 nuns were kidnapped by the rebels.

Then in 2014, the sound of machine guns echoed off the mountains as the rebels, who for months had occupied St Sergius monastery, were driven out by Syrian government forces. During the violence UNESCO world heritage listed churches were burnt, crosses shot at, and Christian villagers held at gun-point, forced to convert to Islam.

Not even this mountain hide-away has been exempt from the horrors of a war that has displaced millions of people and left hundreds of thousands dead, becoming the greatest humanitarian crisis of our times.

The war began in 2011 with a group of school kids and graffiti. Inspired by the 2011 'Arab Spring', which swept across the Middle East in a series of protests and uprisings, a few thirteen-year-old boys from a town in southern Syria thought it would be cool to graffiti a school wall with anti-government slogans.

Detention would have been the humane way to discipline boys with spray cans. But instead the teenagers were arrested, beaten, tortured, and thrown into prison. Citizens demanded the release of the children and peaceful protests began—the people demanded an end to torture, paranoia, and political corruption as they shouted for freedom.

In response to the protests, police fired at the crowds. But the protesters fought back. Soon, a fully-fledged war had erupted between the Assad government and those who called themselves revolutionaries. The conflict quickly snowballed into a complicated war-zone involving foreign parties, each with their own agenda.

The outskirts of Damascus

Eastern Ghouta, just 10 kilometres outside the capital of Damascus, was one of the last strongholds held by the revolutionaries. In February 2018, government forces, backed by Russian warplanes, attacked this heavily populated region with chlorine bombs, barrel bombs and rocket shells. Within days hundreds of civilians had been killed with thousands trapped, starving and without medical assistance. The destruction of Ghouta could be seen from space.

When we read in the Bible about Paul travelling the road to Damascus and encountering the light of heaven, we tend to see ourselves in this account without looking much deeper. We study the Book of Acts and quickly conclude that the same Jesus who revealed himself to Paul has also shone His light into our darkness and saved us. This is a powerful and personal interpretation.

But I like to think that when Jesus met Paul on a road in the Syrian desert, He did so because He foresaw one of the greatest trials our world has ever encountered.

He saw blood and bombs. He heard children's screams. Beheld mother's tears. Longed to comfort tortured and abused souls. And, pined for the rain of His Spirit to soothe this searing Syrian land.

Light from heaven

Two thousand years ago, on the road to Damascus Christ unveiled His light to a man who was on a mission to kill people. On the outskirts of Damascus, Paul gave his heart of hate to Christ, who gave him God's heart of love. And this zealous persecutor of humanity became God's greatest missionary. The Gospel reached the world because God did something radical to one man's heart in…Syria.

There are ancient seeds of Christ planted in Syria. The Book of Genesis reveals God set apart a Syrian woman, Rebekah, to be the mother of Jacob, later named Israel. In the Gospel of Matthew, Jesus heals everyone from Syria who came to Galilee to hear Him preach. Again in Acts we discover that believers were first called Christians in Syria, and it was here that Paul and Barnabas were commissioned by the church to take God's message of salvation to the nations.

Syria is still part of God's plan

For upon a wooden cross of torture, Jesus carried the brokenness of this nation. The Saviour of humanity spilt his Middle Eastern blood, on Middle Eastern sand, for the salvation of every Middle Eastern soul. Such suffering I cannot understand. But I can pray, like Saint Telka, for God to move mountains so His people can find eternal refuge in Him.

May they find a Ma'loula for their souls—a holy 'entrance' into a peace that transcends all understanding.

WHAT WOULD RUSSELL DO?

by Russell Modlin

Six years ago I asked myself this question, and a whole series of questions about who I was and where I was going. I was on the cusp of my 40th birthday and I was ready to enter that next phase of life...whatever that meant! Ready to change states. Ready to change jobs. Ready to pick up my family and move...somewhere else.

I was wondering about the purpose to my journey of following a guy named Jesus. I had been a missionary. A self-funded, non-commissioned and independent missionary. Actually, I just wanted to live the life I knew Jesus wanted me to. Surely, this Christianity thing is able to be lived in the world I was a part of. I really didn't want the labels, but it helped me explain to people why I left Brisbane with my wife and two kids (with one on the way!). It led me to Alice Springs for four years and then eventually led me to the Sunshine Coast.

Six years later I find myself looking in the mirror again at my life. Still teaching secondary students, taking a pay cut to have a 'year off' from a position of leadership, cruising through each school day. Yet, loving every minute of the life I am fortunate enough to lead. I feel I have a smile on my face again. Loving my wife, loving spending time with my sons.

What does God require of me?

If, as a Christian, I fully accepted that God was in control of my life, gave me power to affect change in the world, what would I do? What should I do?

Who would I choose to influence?
Who would I choose to help?

The disciples saw Jesus had power to affect change. They said they were ready to die for Him. They saw lives changed, transformed, healed.

The disciples were following a guy who was saying some pretty crazy things. He was who he said he was, or he was a lunatic. I remember reading what Bono (lead singer of the band U2) had to say about Jesus:

> So what you're left with is: either Christ was who He said He was—the Messiah—or a complete nutcase. I mean, we're talking nutcase on the level of Charles Manson…This man was strapping himself to a bomb, and had "King of the Jews" on his head, and, as they were putting him up on the Cross, was going: OK, martyrdom, here we go. Bring on the pain! I can take it.
>
> I'm not joking here. The idea that the entire course of civilization for over half of the globe could have its fate changed and turned upside-down by a nutcase, for me, that's farfetched…
>
> If only we could be a bit more like Him, the world would be transformed. …When I look at the Cross of Christ, what I see up there is all my @#$% and everybody else's. So I ask myself a question a lot of people have asked: Who is this man? And was He who He said He was, or was He just a religious nut? And there it is, and that's the question. And no one can talk you into it or out of it.

Some of them felt that Jesus was ready to help them take up arms and defeat those who oppressed them.

Some of them were ready to see Jesus become the ruler of Jerusalem or Rome. They were ready to be the ones with the political power and influence.

Some of them were ready to rid the world of corruption, immorality and bring God's judgement onto the world.

They were ready to become the judge and jury. They had been 'out' for so long; now they were 'in'. They now had the 'power' and 'influence' to decide who was 'out' and who was 'in'.

What have 'Christians' done throughout history when they have believed God has given them this power? What good have they done? What evil have they perpetrated?

Yet, Jesus didn't tell them to have the ear of the authorities and influence those with the power. He didn't tell them to 'vote' against Roman rule and take up arms. He didn't tell them to find positions of power in the Roman world to affect change. He didn't tell them to rid the world of those who disagreed with their moral stance, their 'Christian' culture, or their way of life. He didn't tell them to let the world know who was going to hell and who wasn't.

He told them to:

Be a servant
Love enemies
Repent
Forgive
Take the log out of your own eye before you take the speck

out of someone else's.

He said, "Whatever you did for one of the least of these brothers and sisters of mine, you did it for me".

He left us with two 'rules':

Love God
Love Others

What would happen to this world if every morning Russell Modlin arose from his slumber and chose each day to 'Love God' and 'Love Others'?

What would I see?
Who would I see?
Where would I go?

What would Russell do?

BEING IN THE MIDDLE
by Esther Koh

Beginning something is exciting. Ending it is satisfying. The middle, however, is often less desirable. By the time we are in the middle of a marathon we have lost most of the energy we had at the beginning; yet we still have some way to go before reaching the glorious finishing line.

Seasons related to the middle do not attract much positivity either. 'Midlife crisis' and 'middle child syndrome' are things we would like to avoid experiencing. After all, God is the Alpha and Omega, the beginning and the end—but is He the God of the middle too?

The mundane

The thing about being in the middle is this—everything seems slow, or even at a standstill, when we are in the middle of something. At that point of our journey we are usually doing the things we do because we need to and not because we find joy in doing them.

When we begin to pursue our studies, the first year of being an undergraduate is usually fresh and full of new things. University activities, hostel life, and the thrill of finally pursuing our own choice of study fill us with energetic vigour.

As we enter our second year, we begin to settle down and by now have an established routine. We are now familiar with lectures, tutorials, assignments, exams, and other events. Paying rentals and cleaning the hostel becomes a repetitive chore.

If we are not careful, everything starts to become mundane when we are in the middle of the whole process. There is nothing wrong in dutifully fulfilling our commitments and doing what has to be done, but when we are too familiar with it we forget how meaningful things are supposed to be.

When I first became a stay-at-home mum, being able to enjoy breakfast with my son was something I looked forward to! I would eagerly prepare the homemade meals I was not able to make when I was working.

Now, two years later, preparing meals for the family can become more of a necessity than a want. Instead of appreciating what I do for the family, as I used to in the beginning, it has become familiar. While it should still be a privilege to be able to cook for my family, having done it so many times has made me lose enthusiasm; especially as I yearn for something new.

The doing

We are usually driven by what we can do and achieve. Our achievements are often the main representation of who we are. When we are in the middle, there tends to be less doing and action—which is usually unacceptable for us as it reflects unproductivity in our life.

As an English lecturer training teachers-to-be, I felt I was living out God's will in my life as I directed young people to find their purpose. I was challenging them to be the best they could be, knowing they would do the same for their future students.

When I first quit my job to be a stay-at-home mum I enjoyed the time I had with my son and husband. I found joy in finally being a housewife. However, after some time had passed, when I was over the 'newlywed period' of everything being sweet at home, I began to feel like I had lost my purpose in life as I was no longer formally interacting with young people.

My 'doing' was now filled with vacuuming and cleaning the house, washing the laundry, and preparing meals—offering little sense of achievement. There is nothing much to be proud of after completing boring household chores, is there?

Like a student in his second year, I was in the middle of being a stay-at-home mum where all my doings were full of what seemed to be unproductive mundane routines.

The being

However, God is still interested in us, even when we are in the boring middle. This is because we have a God who takes delight in our 'being' more than our 'doing'. When God first created Adam and Eve, He did not create them primarily to be doing things. He made them to have fellowship with Him.

While others look at what we do outwardly, God is more interested with who we are inside. Amazingly, the verse in the middle of the Bible is said to be Psalm 118, verse 8: 'It is better to trust in the Lord than to put confidence in man' (NKJV).

Whether we feel like we are stuck in the middle or are making little progress, God is telling us to trust in Him and not people. We do not have to look to mankind's benchmark of what a successful person must achieve, we should look to what God says about who we are.

I have just crossed the middle mark of my second pregnancy. The buzz of the baby has now died down and there is little activity till we celebrate his arrival. Instead of beating myself down for being unproductive, I choose to invest in all God wants me to be as a mum and wife during this time. This includes enjoying the process of exploring new dishes and keeping the household in order together with my son without being overly stressed about the end product.

So do not fret being in the middle where nothing seems to be happening. God is in control. Always remember, being who God wants you to be in the middle of it all will eventually result in you achieving what God wants you to do in your life.

LOST MY WAY

by Joseph Kolapudi

Have you ever felt like you've been heading in the right direction, but you've just been going about it the wrong way? It can definitely have an effect on the way you see things. This happened to me quite recently.

I was heading to a meeting I knew I was going to be late for, so I absent-mindedly hopped in the car, turned the key in the ignition, and punched in the address on the GPS.

As I turned onto the freeway, my mind drifted to thoughts of what I was going to say at the meeting, and I unconsciously forgot where I was going. After what seemed like half an hour later, I suddenly realised I hadn't the slightest clue where I was. "Where the heck am I?" I wondered aloud.

Frantically reaching for the GPS, I saw that I had taken the longer 'scenic' route to my destination—including a bunch of road work and reduced speed signs picketed along the way.

Needless to say, I was a little frustrated by the delay; but amazingly, I ended up at my destination five minutes ahead of schedule. The meeting went ahead smoothly without the slightest hiccup. All that worrying over nothing, I guess.

Distracted

Oftentimes, we can lose our way at the most inconvenient

of moments. Unforeseen delays, inconceivable frustrations, or unneeded detours can clog our minds and force us to see something that is anything but preferable.

There is an old saying: 'obstacles are what you see when you take your eyes off the goal'. In life, this certainly seems to be the case.

But what causes such distractions? Perhaps it is our ability to get so easily side-tracked by something we fail to realise why we didn't pay attention in the first place. Sometimes, we may even follow someone who tries to be helpful, but in the end does more harm than good. It can be difficult to know what to do in certain situations when everything but the end goal is in sight.

Conquering the challenge

Hiking the highest peak in the San Bernardino mountain range in Southern California isn't the best hike to tackle when you're a first-timer; yet I found myself halfway up Mount Baldy, whose summit is 10, 000 feet above sea level, with the peak hardly in sight.

By now my friends had convinced me to take a 'shortcut' off the hiking trail that seemed to be getting steeper with every step I took. We finally caught sight of the cable car suspended above us, and reckoned we were headed in the right direction.

Suddenly, I realised that the ground beneath us was more porous than I had anticipated, and my boots started sliding downwards. I panicked and fell to my knees, clawing at the rocks just above me.

My friend's hand shot down in front of my face, and I grabbed onto him and collapsed beside him, not a moment too soon. We ended up at the top of the peak in record time, quite grateful that we had made it in one piece.

When incidents that we hadn't planned out take advantage of us, we oftentimes wish we had avoided them at all costs. But isn't overcoming the challenge better than avoiding the challenge entirely? Hindsight often proves so, time and time again.

Life can throw you a curveball, but your strength is proven in the moments of weakness when you choose to stand your ground.

As often as you experience setbacks and struggles, there are moments when you are able to look back and say, 'I made it!'

During those times when you can't see the end in sight, remember that God is still there with you. It is in those moments when we think that we can't turn around or start over that we can trust the One who guides us, even when we lose our way.

HERE AND NOW IN THE INTERLUDE

by Araina Kazia Pereira

It's funny how the Bible, being completed around 1900 years ago, is still the most read book in the world today. Why is it that so many people still read the word even though it was written in ancient history?

Why are we as Christians drawn to reading a book that's written about a time in history that we were never a part of? The answer is simple: the Bible maintains its relevance. It underlines the fundamental truth for all generations—the need for God's love, grace and forgiveness.

Although society has evolved and things that are 'trendy' are constantly changing, God remains unchanged. His Word and His love for His people are constant. Whilst we were not around in the life and times that the Bible was written in, the stories depict a reflection of our own fallen humanity and the promises of God that have and are going to come to pass.

Hebrews chapter 4 verse 12 (ESV) says:

> For the word of God is living and active, sharper than any two-edged sword, piercing to the division of soul and of spirit, of joints and of marrow, and discerning the thoughts and intentions of the heart.

The Bible is written in a unique way. The Old Testament looks at the origin of sin and separation from God; the Israelites, and God's work to bring his people back into relationship with him. Then there is a 400 year long intertestamental period before the New Testament follows the life and death of Jesus, the formation of the early church, and the promise of the Kingdom to come and the return of the Messiah.

Now, as we wait for the return of Christ we are in this period of interlude, awaiting the fulfilment of the prophecies spoken of in Revelation. Yet, this period of interlude is not a passive one, it's not designed to be one of just waiting. And so, Scripture is designed to be fitting for this period.

The Word of God is living and active… provoking us even in the interlude. It is crafted to instil the understanding of God so that we can foster a personal relationship with Him.

Imagine trying to be someone's best friend without knowing a thing about them! You've got to get to know them for them to become your best friend; likewise the Bible gives us the ability to get to know God's nature so that we can grow in relationship with Him. And because God is 'I Am'—unchanging, all-knowing, and loving—the Bible is always going to be relevant and accurate for understanding who God is.

The Bible, whilst crucial to navigating our relationship and journey with God, is not the central point to Christianity. It is not what makes one a Christian. However, it describes the central point to Christianity, Christ. It is through Christ that we are Christian, not simply through owning a Bible—just like we aren't human just because we own a birth certificate or a passport.

Now, not all of Scripture applies to us, such as the Levitical laws or other Old Testament laws. However this is not due to relevancy but simply application of the law and changing times. There is still relevant truth and insight into the nature of God and His will for humanity within those Scriptures.

God is omnipotent, omniscient and omnipresent and His nature as such has been laced throughout Scripture, making it known that He was already aware of future, and the times we are in today. But more importantly our God, described in the Bible is the same God today. The truth of the Gospel remains the same. The word of God still reveals who God is, and what his plans are for humanity. He has still left us with promises to be fulfilled and has commissioned us for His purpose.

The underlying message of the Gospel is the same for all generations; though we are flawed in our human nature, God's grace has saved us, He is faithful, and He wants a relationship with all His people.

Whilst the Bible can tick the boxes for having historical and archaeological merit as well as providing a psychological understanding of human behaviour, its significance is much greater than that. The compilation of Scripture comes from many years and through many people: the prophets who wrote the chapters which formed the Bible. But, while written by them, it was 'God-breathed' (2 Timothy 3:16-17). Inspired by God, and written through those who were in relationship with God and were commissioned to spread the gospel throughout their time and for generations to come.

How can we say this is the case? The promises in the Old Testament were fulfilled over 400 years later in the New Testament. The preservation of ancient texts and finding these Scriptures generations later—couldn't merely have been done by us alone; without God's orchestrating.

So what does this mean for us? Even though times are changing and society is evolving, the truth of the Gospel is still living, relevant to us, and will shape us. We do not need to try to make it relevant by being on 'trend' or following along with society.

The truth of the Gospel is to be told not sold.

We do not need to embellish it to make it relevant. Its relevance comes from the nature of God and His plan for humanity, which is the same today as it was all those years ago.

The interlude however, is simply that. An interlude—an interval or period of time before the next. God's not finished yet.

GET OUT OF YOUR OWN WAY

by Jesse Moore

U2's recent album, Songs of Experience, includes a song titled 'Get Out of Your Own Way'. While listening closely to the creative lyrics I realised how relevant this concept is to my own life, let alone the people around me.

Often, we will find something or someone to blame for situations we've been placed in to avoid facing the harsh reality that it is ourselves that may be our greatest restriction.

The verse that stood out to me most was "Nothing's stopping you except what's inside". Generally, well written music will elicit some sort of image in the listener's mind that helps them put together a story or concept. But, as I listened to the song, I was reminded of a photo that made its way onto my social media news feed a few years back of a fully grown horse tethered to a single leg of a small plastic chair.

Looking at how big this horse was compared to the chair, I wondered why it didn't run away considering one of the horse's legs was three times the size of the chair, which in no way could be a physical restraint.

The horse

So what made this horse think it was actually stuck? A few different answers went through my mind, such as the possibility that it was just well-trained and loyal to its owner—which could very well have been true. However, for the sake of this analogy we will assume that the horse was just so used to the idea of being tethered to something solid that it never realised the real tether was its mind. Similarly, we can be weighed down by things that have no physical weight, such as something from the past that seems inescapable. In that case, the only way it has power is if it's granted power.

Power is often given to thoughts that sabotage self worth, such as, "I'm not good enough", and "There are people more qualified than me for that position". It's interesting to note that these thoughts that make us feel like less of a person are attached to fear almost every time.

A desire for change

Another angle from this song could relate to the desire for change. Whether it's personal change like joining a gym or changing jobs, or social change like a political movement or demanding action against some injustice, there is always a time for change. Often, you can see posts on social media by people who are upset with a political outcome or social injustice who finds the energy to rant to everyone about it with little action attached. But, maybe the solution is with you, and maybe the issue is less about the problem and more about one's failure to act on it.

Sometimes we are our biggest problem, but we may also be our biggest solution—so long as we're able to see it. Instead of getting in the way of ourselves and blocking the view of what might be, perhaps we should move ourselves out of the way and see just how far the horizon is.

A YOUNG HORSE IS NO GOOD UNTIL HE'S STARTED

by John Skinner

Over the years I've broken-in quite a few young horses, what we now call 'starting' a colt.

No matter how quiet they are, how precious, how gentle, how pretty, the young horse needs to learn some lessons because, as he stands there in the paddock, he's no good to anyone except to look at.

First off, he needs to learn I won't hurt him so I rub him all over, it feels pretty good, you know—like a massage. Then he needs to learn some manners like don't kick, don't push, don't turn your back on me, don't touch me until I touch you, lift your feet off the ground when I ask for it, and more.

Unless I can get him to this basic stage, he's not worth having around the place—he's no good to anyone.

Leading

Now, the young horse needs to learn to lead so he goes where I go and when I go, then, perhaps the most important early lesson, to tie up and not pull back trying to break the rope or his own neck.

Once we've successfully reached this stage, we can start the 'mouthing' process. It's not easy and many horses fight and struggle, some stand in the corner and sulk, but it's not over until the horse learns to bend its neck, accept the bit and 'give' its head, that is, take pressure off the bit in its mouth.

We're now through this stage and it's time to move into teaching the horse to lunge, that is walk, trot and lope in a circle, small ones right out to big ones, to pay attention to what I'm asking it to do, and pick up the right lead for the direction its going. Yes, there's some horse talk here you may not understand but you soon get my drift—the colt is learning some lessons.

Now it's time to put a saddle on the horse's back if you haven't already done so. This is usually at the end of the first week, or perhaps 10 days depending on how easily the colt learnt its lessons.

This is where the 'rubber hits the road' and we find out just how quiet he really is. Does he buck, run off scared, lie down and sulk, or just accept what is being done? I've seen all these scenarios.

Next we start putting these lessons into place at the same time.

He has his head tied back a little, he is made walk, trot and lope while lunging with the saddle on his back, picking up his correct leads, and he has to be watching me because I'm the boss, the master as far as he's concerned.

How do you know a horse is paying attention to you? It's all in his ears. The one closest to you should be facing toward the boss (the open part towards you).

Some people will tie all sorts of things to the saddle about now, bags of rattling cans, long saddle rugs or raincoats, plastic bags, lengths of rope, all things which the horse will learn to accept once he realises these things don't hurt. Personally, I don't like to frighten a youngster; I'll do one or two of these things when I'm riding him at some stage in the future.

Then comes the next step—step-up, that is—and into the saddle. My experience is, don't do this on your own. When he gets used to you being above him, your exaggerated movements in the saddle, getting on and off both sides, sliding over his rump, he's right to start moving off. And, if he gets that right, he's ready to be outside the yard.

Once he can handle being ridden among the trees and rocks, he's about to graduate kindergarten. This is only achieved through time (three to four weeks, though some will take longer, and others are ready in two), patience, perseverance, kindness, and a knowledge of what to do to overcome all the little obstacles the youngster places in your way.

Young Christians, and I'm not talking about age here, are so full of enthusiasm they sometimes want to save the whole world in a week but; just like the young horse, there's lessons to be learnt and stages to go through to be truly effective.

Jesus took three years to teach his disciples what he wanted them to learn and he was a 'Master' teacher. We too, need to learn the basics or we will just stand in the paddock where we are only good to look at.

Our lessons start with Bible knowledge. Read your Bible first and foremost, read recommended books, listen to teachers, your elders, and to experienced Christians who have borne fruit.

Most of all, 'give' your head to Christ, bridle your tongue, accept heavy burdens when asked, be aware of obstacles placed in your path, know that patience and perseverance only come through trials. But, also learn that your Heavenly Father is kind, loves you and will not give you a trial or burden you cannot handle.

My horse has now become a useful animal to me. Yes, he still has heaps to learn, in fact he'll never stop learning—but then neither should I.

We all start out as young colts (or fillies) in Christ and we should never stop learning.

CONVENIENT CROSS
by Petro Swart

The Microwave Generation. It is sadly the reality we are living in, flavoured with entitlement, self-satisfaction and impatience. I think we can all freely admit that we have all bought into the culture of instant satisfaction. Lime scooters, UberEats, and the looming 5G network were all created to speed up our lives and make satisfying our desires easier.

While there is certainly nothing sinful about convenience or ease, I believe it becomes an issue when it becomes an idol.

Comfort disguised as fear

A speaker at a conference once explained her journey with surrendering her comfort idol. She used the example of wanting to stay in pyjamas at home rather than go out and disciple girls as God had called her to—constantly prioritising her comfort over serving in the Kingdom.

I think what we often label as fear is actually unwillingness to be uncomfortable. We say that we are reluctant to get out of our comfort zone because of fear of failure, rejection, or embarrassment, when the truth is that we may just be fearing the feeling of discomfort.

Shaking hands, the metallic taste in your mouth, jelly legs, and a suddenly thick tongue characterise a crippling fear. Or do they represent discomfort? Is it that these symptoms can be present in both situations, the reason that we categorise our feelings wrong? Or is it something else?

"Success is never achieved in your comfort zone"

As addicted as we are as a generation to convenience, so are we to success. We have, however, lost the willingness to work for that success. Everyone is looking for a 'get-rich-quick' scheme—the emphasis being on quick. As with everything in our instant-satisfaction saturated lives, we demand instant success. Comfort is treated the same.

Comfort is not something that we are willing to work for, it is something that we see as being an innate human right. Let me be clear, I am not talking about comforts such as running water, warm shelter and enough to eat—those should be accessible for all people. I am addressing that self-satisfying comfort where all your needs are constantly, instantly met.

Treat yo'self

Self-care is a hot topic—first the message was stressing the importance of it, then how to apply it, and most recently I have been seeing many articles popping up about potentially overdoing it. I think we can all agree that a treat, by definition, is an occasional occurrence. When we treat ourselves too often, the treat loses its value as a 'treat'.

A massage. That is my idea of an ultimate treat. But, now imagine that every time I woke up with a stiff neck or sore muscles I booked a pre-work massage. Not only would I find myself broke pretty quickly, but I would not appreciate the value of saving up for a decent pillow, or the knowledge that my sore muscles mean I am getting stronger from exercising. Massages would probably lose their novelty as well.

In the same way, comfort has become our idea of a constant state of being—a right, not a treat.

Why comfort must stay a treat

If success is gained outside of our comfort zone, and we grow when we are pushed and stretched, why would we want to live in a state of comfort?

Living in comfort means that success and growth would only occur occasionally and in small doses—almost like a treat. The difference is, though, that we would never seek out a time of feeling uncomfortable to treat ourselves. Therefore, we would be stagnant and mildly unsuccessful.

In contrast, if we are more often uncomfortable, we will be learning and achieving while still seeking out times to be comfortable. That's a more sustainable and successful lifestyle, right?

The biblical basis of discomfort

God's heart is not for us to suffer, but as a good Father He knows that we must learn and grow. As Creator, He knows that our world is not perfect, and that sanctification is a process. While God has proven Himself time and time again as rescuer, Saviour, warrior and a safe shelter, He never promises the easy road.

Jesus says:

> "Come to me, all you who are weary and burdened, and I will give you rest. Take my yoke upon you and learn from me, for I am gentle and humble in heart, and you will find rest for your souls. For my yoke is easy and my burden is

light." (Matthew 11, verses 28-30 NIV).

He also says:

> Then Jesus told his disciples, "If anyone would come after me, let him deny himself and take up his cross and follow me. For whoever would save his life will lose it, but whoever loses his life for my sake will find it. For what will it profit a man if he gains the whole world and forfeits his soul? Or what shall a man give in return for his soul?" (Matthew 16 verses 24-26 ESV)

In order to follow Jesus, we must deny ourselves. He promises that His burden is light, but He does not promise that there will be no burden. Sanctification and following Jesus is easy and light because it comes from a place of humility and knowing that becoming more like Christ comes hand-in-hand with peace and joy—regardless of our circumstances.

This principle applies to our purity, speech, thoughts and conduct—it will not always be convenient, comfortable and easy to walk in purity and truth. As with success, we will not be sanctified by remaining in our comfort zones. Therefore, in grey area decisions it is always important to question whether the immediately self-satisfying path is the correct decision based on 'rights' or truth.

Do not fear making the unpopular decision. Do not avoid being uncomfortable because of that stance that you have taken. Do not expect instant sanctification.

Let us not buy into the microwave generation expectations, but instead pick up our crosses, and wear God's yoke with humility and joy. Let us deny our desire for instant comfort, and work towards sanctification.

SINGING THROUGH THE SHADOWS

by Rebecca Howan

Mental illness. It's not something we like to talk about, and yet the number of people who battle with their mental wellbeing is extremely high.

I've struggled with anxiety on and off for the past three years, but the last few months have definitely been more 'on' than off. While I wouldn't say that it's been the most severe episode I've experienced, my mind has still been in a constant underlying state of fear and worry for months.

Sometimes it rears its head for a few hours or a few days and completely consumes my thoughts, and sometimes it just sits in the back of my mind, passive but palpable, biding its time before the next trigger. No matter the severity, though, the symptoms are still there in varying degrees—loss of appetite, shivers, not being able to sleep, nausea, exhaustion, and numbness. I know that anxiety is often irrational, but its effects on my body are real.

Crying out to God

The thing that I'm finding the hardest is the sense that God has somehow betrayed me. Where are you, God? When you love me so much, why do you let me feel like this? When you have the power to break me free from this, why do you let me suffer? When you've placed a calling ahead of me that feels impossible when anxiety is raging, why do you not take it away?

Thankfully, I think these questions are natural and God honestly doesn't mind when we ask them. After all, the Psalms are full of these exact same thoughts! There are countless instances of David, the man after God's own heart no less (Acts chapter 13, verse 22), crying out in desperation to God.

I do find it interesting that in the Church, people's response in time of anxiety or depression is often to suggest that we need to pray more, have more faith, or rely more on the truth of the Scriptures. While I know that these suggestions are often genuine and heartfelt, they are also largely not helpful. Why do we assume that someone struggling with mental wellbeing is not doing these things? Would we suggest that David's desperate cries in the Psalms were because he didn't pray enough?

The Psalms are so wonderful for this reason, displaying the full showcase of human emotion against the backdrop of faith. And so I take comfort in the fact that in the Psalms, and for generations since, people have been crying out to God with exactly the same cries as mine. But, more than that, I take comfort in the fact that in all these situations, the cries are followed by praise, and that faith and hope prevail every time.

Choosing to worship

One of my favourites throughout the years has been Psalm chapter 42. It is so raw with heartbreak and desperation and yet in the face of this, the writer repeatedly makes the conscious decision to praise:

> Why, my soul, are you downcast? Why so disturbed within me? Put your hope in God, for I will yet praise him, my Saviour and my God. (Psalm chapter 42, verse 5 NIV).

Though I'm in the midst of this dark season, I've been challenged and inspired to still choose to praise and to sing through these shadows. Even though I can't see the end at the moment, I choose to worship nonetheless, because God is worthy to be praised for who He is—good and holy.

But I also choose to worship him for what He has already done, because He has shown His faithfulness to the people who have gone before, like David in the Psalms, and I know that he will show his faithfulness to me.

Breakthrough is coming

"Worship is the prelude; it becomes before the testimony".

I heard Brian Houston say this at one of Hillsong's Worship and Creative Conferences, and it has truly resonated with me ever since. Not only will I choose to worship for who God is and for what He has done, but for what I know He is going to do!

I worship with faith and expectation and confidence that breakthrough will come. I worship in the knowledge that my testimony is coming. I worship because I know that despite my anxious thoughts, God will empower and enable me for the calling He's placed ahead of me.

There's always a reason to worship, so I continue to make

a conscious decision to praise, and to keep singing through the shadows.

PRAYER, THE MOST INTIMATE CONVERSATION

by Kevin Park

Mouths are not only for taste but they are also for initiating conversations.

When we get together with family members and close friends, we love to converse with one another. Without conversation, we lead unfulfilled lives.

Therefore, a conversation is one of the most important ways to build a relationship with one another.

Prayer

Like daily conversations between people, prayer is the way to have a conversation with God.

God longs to communicate with every one of us because we automatically become His children if we believe in Jesus Christ. More than that, prayer builds the bridge between Heaven and Earth.

Prayer is like spiritual oxygen, however, it can be easy to ignore in today's busy culture. It feels counterintuitive to stop in the middle of something and fix our eyes on God, whom we cannot physically see and hear, and lay our needs before Him.

We naturally desire to attempt everything ourselves. When

we do think to pray in a roundabout way, we are often asking God for an easy and comfortable life. We may pretend that our expression to God is real devotion towards Him while our motivation is focused on ourselves.

Although being a good provider is a part of God's job, He desires to see our surrendered devotion towards Him. Throughout the New Testament, Jesus Christ illustrated His devotion to God.

Since Christ was partly human when He came to earth, He did not want to suffer so He pleaded with His Father three times that suffering may be taken from Him. However, He suffered to the point of His death, anyway.

We may wonder why He chose to suffer, instead of protecting Himself with God's power. It was all because of His devotion towards His Father. Jesus' mission was to fulfil God's mission, which was sacrificing Himself for our salvation (Matthew chapter 26, verses 36-56).

Lord's Prayer

Before Jesus was crucified, He taught His followers how to pray. In Matthew's Gospel, they were taught not to be like hypocrites who pray with fancy words or to impress others.

Although prayer should be a heartfelt conversation, the Lord's prayer is an important guide. It includes not only simple instructions on how to pray, but it is also based on God's mission.

The Lord's Prayer teaches us how to align ourselves with God's will. We know this, especially because the first acknowledgement is an honour to God's authority. Following this, it asks that His kingdom may be visible on earth with a surrendered heart.

> 'Mission arises from the heart of God Himself, and is communicated from His heart to ours.' (John Stott, The Contemporary Christian: An Urgent Plea for Double Listening)

The Priority of Prayer

Prayer is a spiritual practice we should treasure and never take for granted. We need God all the time, every day and every second.

Through God's spoken word, the universe was made; more specifically heavens and the earth. Something humans will never be able to achieve.

While He is in charge of everything on Heaven and Earth and remains flawless, we continue to stumble in many ways. God knows every detail of our lives, from beginning to end.

Jesus knew the priority of prayer. He valued prayer above everything else.

In Mark chapter 11, verses 15-17, Jesus saw money changers at the temple and overthrew everything and proclaimed, "Is it not written: 'My house will be called a house of prayer for all nations?' But you have made it 'a den of robbers.'"

While there are many valuable things for the church, prioritising prayer is recognised as valuing God above all else. If prayer is not a priority, everything will be crumbling down according to Jesus.

I love being in prayer ministries, such as an E-Prayer Lead, and a prayer calendar facilitator. They motivate me to pray for my church. Most of all, prayer motivates us to fellowship with our heavenly Father.

I do not have to get all my words right in prayer as it is Jesus who is the true intercessor (Romans chapter 8, verses 26-27, 34).

> God has strategically chosen to establish and utilise prayer as part of His sovereign plan for us. It is like oxygen to our spiritual lives. It provides the needed wind in our sails to propel everything we do as believers, and it's the unseen key to the success of every ministry of the church.
> (Alex and Stephen Kendrick)

So, let us clear spaces to pray for one another and, most importantly, to have intimate fellowship with God, our heavenly Father. I know I have to!

FINDING FREEDOM

by Matthew Thornton

Recently I was asked to share at my church's youth camp. The topic was an easy one: how has Jesus impacted your life?

I say it was easy because there are so many things I could have talked about. But there was one word that kept coming back to my mind: freedom.

Now, of course, freedom from sin is generally the first thought that comes to mind when we think about Jesus. But, for me, Jesus' freedom extends to more than just sin. He gives me freedom from my mind and my emotions as well.

Alleviating anxiety

You see, when I was younger, I used to really battle with worry and anxiety. Often, I would find myself in a place where I was just overwhelmed by it. I was mostly worried about the future—frightened by it to be more honest. Specifically, I was scared of what the potential effects of my failures—particularly at school—would have on my future.

I knew God had a plan for me, and that it was a good plan. But I often thought I would mess it up if I were to make the wrong decision or not succeed in something I was 'supposed to'. Unfortunately, this thinking brought another emotion into the mix—regret.

Not only was I scared that I might do something in the future to mess it up, but I would also lament over past decisions that I was sure negatively impacted my trajectory. I was hindered by the past and intimidated by the future. But there is an iconic verse that has changed my life. It is Romans chapter 8, verse 28: 'In all things God works for the good of those who love Him'.

To me, the key to this verse are the words: "for those who love Him". Because, what this told me is that—provided my heart is inclined to Him, and my intention is to do His will in my life—the word regret and mistake don't exist.

The fear of making mistakes came from the belief that their effects would be irreversibly negative in my life. How comforting to know then that any mistake could be made into something good by Him.

Greater than all my regrets

With God, mistakes aren't dead ends, but an opportunity for Him to re-route. You're not sure about something? You don't know where to step next? Pray to God. Seek His will. Then do what you think He is saying is right. Whatever you choose, you aren't disqualifying God's plan for you. He will use whatever decision you make for good.

When it comes to regret, God is greater than all our regrets. It's the title of one of my favourite songs by Tenth Avenue North and some of it goes:

> So if I fall and if I fail,
> I will trust Your mercy is
> Greater than all of this
> And if I bend and if I break

> I'll trust the hands that hold me are
> Greater than all my regrets
> You are greater than all my regrets

As the lead singer puts it: "Regret is the belief that the mess I made can't be made into something beautiful by Him".

It all comes back to having faith in that verse. Because that verse contains a truth—and I'm sorry if it hurts your ego—you simply aren't capable of making a mess He can't fix. What an amazing comfort.

Trust-falling

So, how has Jesus changed my life? Well, He came to bring freedom and He certainly did. He gives me freedom from my past—my regrets, my mistakes—and He gives me freedom from the future. I don't have to worry because He works in all things for good. I have freedom from what has gone before, and I have freedom from what is to come...and this allows me to find joy in what is happening now.

> Trust is believing your future is wrapped in the love of God, and if that's the case, then we can trust-fall into wherever God leads. – (Mike Donehey, Finding God's Will for my Life)

That joy is available to each and everyone one of us. Whether it's the future or the past that is taking hostage of your mind, give it to God. Trust that He will work it for good. He has never let me down—and I promise He won't let you down either.

YOU RUN WITH HORSES NOW

by Amy Manners

I once dreamt of Elijah running with the horses. The stallions' manes were swept back in the fierce gallop, and with each thundering stride their muscles rippled beneath glistening coats, like silk swaying in the wind.

Hooves hit the dry earth of a drought-sick land, flicking up a cloud of dust. And from the wild herd emerged Elijah, running with a strength not his own. He looked ahead with determination, focus, and an inner knowing that rain was coming in answer to his prayers. The rise and fall of his steps matched the rhythm of the spirited beasts as the sky clouded over with heavy showers. A Scripture rumbled through me as I slept:

> If you get tired racing against people, how can you race against horses? (Jeremiah, chapter 12, verse 5 NCV)

I knew Elijah had long left the races of men behind, he was racing with horses now, and this was my call to do the same.

A holy misfit

I woke from that dream trying to catch the pace of Elijah's race. The prophet was one who ran, not to please men, but to please God.

Elijah didn't care what people thought. If he did, he wouldn't have approached the throne of King Ahab's immoral government and prophesied a drought, hardly a crowd-pleasing sermon. But one he hoped would shake his people out of living for themselves and return to their true calling to be Children of God. After preaching, Elijah was greeted, not with applause, but instead the sword. He was so unpopular he had to run for his life.

Eliyahu in Hebrew simply means 'My God is Yahweh'. This was Elijah's sole identity and purpose: his God was the LORD. When everyone else was partying with foreign gods and living for the lusts of fading pleasures, Elijah obeyed God's orders to care for a non-Israeli widow during the drought and famine—this definitely wasn't a fashionable thing to do. But Elijah wasn't running his race to fit in, he ran to stand out for the right reasons. He ran with his eyes upon an eternal prize: the One who outlives the dust of droughts and jeers of men.

Elijah ran simply to bring delight to God. Though the race was hard, he didn't give up.

Rains of change

> Elijah said, "...Rain is on the way; I hear it coming".
> ...[He] climbed to the top of Carmel, bowed deeply in prayer, his face between his knees. Then he said to his young servant, "On your feet now! Look toward the sea". He went, looked, and reported back, "I don't see a thing."
> "Keep looking", said Elijah, "seven times if necessary".
> And sure enough, the seventh time he said,
> "Oh yes, a cloud! But very small, no bigger than someone's hand, rising out of the sea."
> "Quickly then, on your way. Tell Ahab, 'Saddle up and get down from the mountain before the rain stops you.'"
> Things happened fast. The sky grew black with wind-

driven clouds, and then a huge cloudburst of rain, with Ahab hightailing it in his chariot for Jezreel. And God strengthened Elijah mightily. Pulling up his robe and tying it around his waist, Elijah ran in front of Ahab's chariot until they reached Jezreel.
(1 Kings chapter 18, verse 41-46 MSG)

Upon the heights of Mount Carmel, Elijah bowed with knees pressed to the barren dust and prayed for rain. He prayed while the skies were empty, the ground was dry and the famine at it severest point. He prayed because prayer was the only thing that could break the drought. Even when circumstances appeared unchanged, he dared to hear, by faith, the sound of abundant rain.

Time after time Elijah's servant looked out to sea only to deliver the same report: nothing had changed. The sky was still empty, the earth a dust-heap, and stomachs hungry.

Yet somewhere beyond the horizon, out of sight, moisture gathered above the ocean. On the seventh time, the servant saw the faintest whisper of a cloud rising over the horizon.

Keep praying

"Great blessings often come from small beginnings, and showers of plenty from a tiny cloud." —Matthew Henry

When you pray and circumstances appear unchanged, take heart—somewhere beyond your horizon the rains of change are stirring, lifting, growing. You might not see it yet, but know the prayer-cloud is rising. When you glimpse the faintest appearance of that cloud, you'll know it's time to run. For your sky will soon be shrouded with the downpour of answered prayer.

Showers of plenty will soak your parched land and your weary earth will give birth to promises long buried.

So, run like Elijah. Run with strength that's not your own, run ahead of earthly chariots in all their fading glory, run in humility towards an eternal prize, run because your God has carried you this far and He's not letting go.

As you leave the unfulfilling races of people-pleasing behind, you'll hear the thundering hooves of a holy purpose resounding.

Yes, you run with horses now.

Section three

Family, Friends and the Body of Christ

GOOD FRIENDS ARE GOOD FOR THE SOUL

by Rebecca Howan

How amazing are friends? It's really struck me over these past few weeks just how immensely grateful I am for the friends that God has placed in my life. They have been so instrumental in helping me to become who I am today, and over the past few months I have been reminded again and again just how much they mean to me.

Deep Heart and Soul Connection

While all friends are great, though, not all friendships are created equal. I don't say that to be mean or exclusive, but to emphasise that there is a certain kind of friendship that is sacred and holy, a friendship that is good for your soul.

I'm not talking about surface-level friends, those who catch up for coffee once in a while, who see each other at mutual gatherings, or who swap notes once a week on what's happened on their favourite tv show.

I'm talking about friends with a deep heart and soul connection. I'm talking about friends who tell each other everything, who encourage each other with kind words and challenge each other with hard words. I'm talking about friends who have no judgement, and who you tell your deepest darkest secrets to in the knowledge that they'll still love you and journey with you. I'm talking about friends who weep together and who rejoice together. I'm talking about friends that help you to be the best version of yourself, the person that God designed you to be.

Is there anything sweeter in this world than friendships like this?

I pray that you know exactly what I'm talking about because you have friends like this too. These friends are precious. They are absolute treasures, blessings from heaven above, and they should not be taken for granted.

Created for community

The beautiful thing about these friendships is that this is exactly how God designed it to be. We are not meant to do life alone. God has created us for community, and this is the way of Jesus, the way of the Kingdom.

I'm an off-the-chart extrovert and so I do have some bias when it comes to believing in the importance of friendships, but even the biggest introverts need close and godly friends.

There are so many examples of great friendships in the Bible—David and Jonathan, Moses and Aaron, Naomi and Ruth. The story of David and Jonathan's friendship in 1 Samuel chapter 18 is particularly beautiful, with a deep emotional bond, fierce loyalty, and personal sacrifices made for the other. To read through their friendship and journey is so profound—oh, what a blessing to have a friendship like theirs!

Three reasons good friends are good for the soul

There are countless reasons that these godly friendships are good for our souls. Friends are great for holding you accountable. When there is a close friendship, there are no qualms in calling you out and telling you when you're being selfish, when you're overreacting, when you've picked up a bad behaviour or stopped doing a good one, or if you're simply just acting completely out of line. The beauty of this is that there is a mutual understanding these rebukes and challenges are offered because they have your best interests at heart, and they want you to be the best person you can be.

Friends can also pray for you when you can't pray for yourself. Over the years, I've had seasons of doubt, seasons of anxiety and depression, and seasons of downright anger with God. In these seasons, it's often hard to get on my knees and bring my requests to God, even though I know in my head that that's exactly what I should do. This is where good friends can come in and bring the cries of your heart to God on your behalf, where you can't yourself.

Finally, there's nothing worse than feeling like you have to put on a mask and hold it in when you're having a horrific season, just out of courtesy for the other people around you. But good friends can weep with you when you're weeping. There are no formalities or niceties in a friendship like this, but we can be our vulnerable and true selves with each other, whether that means weeping when times are bad, or rejoicing when times are good.

Share the love

If this rings true for you and you have friends like this, share the love with them and let them know how dearly you appreciate them. But if this has caused a pang in your heart because you don't have any friends like this in this season, perhaps pray to God to bring some godly friends into your life.

Because everyone deserves a friend that is truly good for your soul.

TRAIN BRAKES
by John Skinner

Apart from working in shearing sheds and doing cattle work further west, the NSW Government Railways was my first job after school.

My dad spent 40 years in the railway after leaving the family dairy farm and what he didn't know about steam, diesel and electric engines probably wasn't worth knowing.

One of the most important lessons he ever gave me concerned the Westinghouse braking system which was consistent on trains throughout NSW.

It was pretty normal to have goods (freight) trains weighing about 1200 tonnes and, when they reach normal travelling speed of 100k/h, they can take several kilometres to stop. Can you just imagine the phenomenal speed to weight ratio?

However, many years ago, the NSW Railways adopted the Westinghouse system which was exactly opposite to what most other railways were using at the time. It was compressed air, just as they all were, but the Westinghouse system didn't apply the brakes by increasing pressure, the brakes were applied by releasing the pressure.

Manual Application

This was also very safe. If the compressor were to breakdown, the brakes would start to apply as soon as the air pressure fell.

Should the other system fail, the only way to stop was to manually apply the brakes.

The train driver had control of the braking system with a gauge to keep him informed of the air pressure. When the air pressure started falling, he would soon see there was a problem. Just the same, when he needed to stop the train it was a matter of a controlled reduction of air pressure.

In time, almost all railway systems throughout the world started using the Westinghouse system.

Broken airlines

For the system to be effective, every carriage or goods truck had to be coupled with an airline, right to the back which, in my day, was a guard's van.

Should an air hose coupling break between carriages or trucks (the coupling was intentionally the weakest point), the train would slowly creep to a stop and a spare hose was needed—in those days, all engines carried spares and it was usually the fireman's job to replace the problem coupling.

A leak in an air hose posed the same problem—as the air escaped, the brakes came on.

The driver's experience with the braking system and with compressor settings was a necessity. No-one became a driver until they'd had years of experience as the fireman or what they now call, the observer.

In order for the train to keep going, all the airline couplings must stay together and not break or leak, lest the whole train stops.

It's like us as a Church (or body of Christ), unless we're on the same track and all working together, the whole process can slowly grind to a stop.

Jesus is our 'compressed air' and while ever He's powering us, all is fine until something or someone breaks and the 'air' leaks out.

Jesus has the knowledge and experience to keep our train on track and keep it moving forward so if there is a problem, He's the one we need to ask about fixing it.

RELIGION VERSES RELATIONSHIP

by Jo Fuller

Religiosity and its regimental rules and regulations ties us up in chains and keeps us in bondage. It can trap us in fear; causing us to rely on our self and our own efforts to save us.

Religion barks orders to their slaves, keeping us thinking, "when I have done this or accomplished that or have cleaned myself up, only then could I possibly please and gain acceptance from God".

Religion is the opposite of intimate relationship with our Creator—the kind He yearns to have with us.

Relationship

Relationship, at its core is based in Love. A love like no other. A love that has no conditions attached to it, a love that knows no bounds. A love that accepts.

Relationship with the One seeks to know, listen and please Him out of wanting to, rather than out of duty. Relationship is anchored in Grace and knows, "I don't have to be perfect to come running into the safety and shelter of His arms".

Relationship is freedom, colourful and liberating. Religion is restrictive, grey and debilitating.

The Path to Relationship

> I am the way and the truth and the life. No one comes to the Father except through me. (John chapter 14 verse 6 NIV)

Jesus is the Way to intimate relationship. Recognising we need a saviour, repenting and returning to Him sets us on the right path.

Then we can come boldly into his presence, as a child boldly runs to their parent; unashamed, uninhibited and free.

Oh, how He yearns for this closeness, this intimacy. For us to tell Him everything and to just sit in His presence. To know who we are as a child of God, to know He sees us without spot or blemish; because when He sees us, He sees His Son (1 Corinthians chapter 5, verses 17-21).

This precious gift has nothing to do with our self-effort and what a relief that is.

> For by grace we have been saved through faith, and that not of ourselves; it is the gift of God. (Ephesians chapter 2, verse 8 NIV)

Let us continue to seek His face and present ourselves as living sacrifices for Him (Romans chapter 12, verse one).

Relationship to Rule

Give us eyes to see as you see,
give us ears to hear, as you do.
May the scales fall off our eyes,
may we hear the broken-hearted cries.

Help us live out our God-given destinies,
to abide in you and to rest.
To know your heart and mind,
our Heavenly Father—merciful, loving and kind.

HOW GOD TURNED MY LONELINESS FROM A BURDEN INTO A BLESSING

(Romans 8:28 lived out)
by Jessica McPherson

One movie I really enjoy is *My Big Fat Greek Wedding*. I love the idea of a huge family where everyone is really close and there is always food and festivity happening! There are obviously downsides to this as well (that the main character struggles with!) but I still love the idea of such a warm, close-knit community!

The Desire for Friendship

I have a great family but it is also a very small family. When I was five, we moved away from the region where our extended family live to go to Greymouth and then later on, Christchurch. I had one sister (who is amazing) but she left home when I was 12 because she is six and a half years older than me and she was going to study in Dunedin. When I was at high school I didn't really have friends and didn't really fit in anywhere.

However, God gifted me with a strong personality and convictions so most of the time I didn't mind not being popular or having friends, but I did long for the kind of relationships I read about in books that involved constant phone calls, sleepovers, and secret sharing; for friends who would plan surprises and celebrations for me and who I could do the same for.

Now as an adult I am making up for lost time and have so many wonderful friendships that bring so much joy to my life including my very best friend—my husband Eoin! I am so happy to have so many great friendships now but I also really valued my earlier experiences because looking back I can see how God used them to shape me and bring good from them!

God's Greater Plan!

Romans chapter 8, verse 28 says,

> And we know that for those who love God all things work together for good, for those who are called according to his purpose. (ESV)

This verse is in a passage that talks about suffering, endurance, and future hope; it is not talking simply about how God will give us good things (even though he does!) but it is talking about how, even in bad situations, God can bring good out of them for His people.

If you had asked me when I was a teenager whether I wanted a group of close friends to share high school with, I would have said 'Yes!' but then I would have missed out on what I have learnt from the experience of being lonely and desiring special, close, friendships. Today, one of the things that makes me saddest is people who feel lonely, insignificant, left out, or picked on. There are few things that wring my heart as much as the idea that someone doesn't have friends (or sometimes even family!) who make them feel like they're special. I feel I have deep wells of empathy which I can draw upon (and do without even thinking) because I have had the experience of lacking friendship.

One of my goals in life is to make sure no one around me lacks someone to celebrate them, tell them they're special, befriend them, and generally make them feel loved! Since I know what it is like to experience this and desire this, I feel like it is easier to spot that in other people and be able to come alongside them. It is like God has given me radar vision for people who need someone to love them!

The Blessing of the Church Family

When I came to university I started attending a new church and I really came to understand the depth and breadth of the church family and how much of a gift it is! I came to understand how the church family is just like our immediate family—God puts you there and you are meant to stick with them through thick and thin—it is both challenging and incredibly encouraging. Being in a church that really emphasises the responsibility and joy of being joined together in the body of Christ has fulfilled more of childhood longings, especially since our church has such a diverse range of people from all over the world! I have been given the huge, warm, close-knit family I dreamed of!

How has God shaped you?

I want to finish on the question of how has God shaped you? What experiences have you had that at the time you would have gladly traded away but are now grateful for? How have they impacted your life and how have they turned you into the person you are today? Sometimes it takes a chance to pause and reflect to be able to see how God has used a sad experience and turned it into a good outcome, but if we take the time to look then I believe we will see that, as Paul says in Romans, 'And we know that for those who love God all things work together for good, for those who are called according to his purpose'.

EVERYONE HAS A SUPERPOWER

by Kristen Dang

Superpowers come in many shapes and sizes. There are the heroes who wield thunder, fire, water and otherworldly weapons. There are also the heroes cast into their role; overcomers who learn to conquer their fears and lay themselves down to protect others. Many heroes keep their identity secret. Day to day, they work or study inconspicuously amongst others, while also keeping watch for any signs of danger.

We watch them on the movie screens, celebrate their victories, and look forward to being part of their next adventure. These heroes are fictional characters with imagined superpowers, but what of the superpowers we can see everyday?

Gifted with power

Everyone has a superpower. We might not fly or shoot fire from our hands, but we have all been fearfully and wonderfully made in the image of Christ, given different spiritual gifts as the Holy Spirit distributes.

> But one and the same Spirit works all these things, distributing to each one individually as He wills.
> (1 Corinthians chapter 12, verse 11 NKJV)

We might not all do the same ministry, speak to the same people, or testify of God in the same manner, but we have all been equipped with power through the Holy Spirit with individual spiritual gifts that help us do what God has called us to do on this earth.

Yes, we have a calling. Yes, we have a purpose. Yes, we have identity as children of God, as partakers in His glory, as co-heirs with Christ, and as victorious warriors in His army. He chooses us to speak His truth and His love to those around us. He chooses us to use the blessings and grace He gives us to lift up the hurting and broken-hearted. He chooses us to stand for righteousness in the face of injustice, and to hold up His banner of love in a world that shoots arrows of hate, loneliness and pain.

He demonstrated His love when He died on the cross for us, and demonstrated His victory when He rose from the grave. He calls us to lay down our lives in complete surrender to Him so that He can work through us to breathe life into this world.

Our ultimate superpower is faith in Christ—the One through whom all things are possible.

The church: a team of superpowered people

It was a mid-week gathering and the speaker was just about to start. I looked at the people around me; everyone worshipping, everyone ready to listen to the word of God. Here in this small room, I saw many gifts at work, and was reminded of how God's blessings can be experienced in so many different ways.

There stood an encourager, actively lifting others up and giving them opportunities to step out in faith and develop their God-given talents. There sat a gentle servant, always looking to help in any way possible, faithfully and joyfully serving without any need for self-recognition. There with lifted hands was a shepherd, diligent to protect others from harm, and eager to feed them with the goodness of God's word. There with heaven-turned face, was a prayer warrior unafraid to cry out to the Lord on behalf of others.

There they worshipped; administrators, teachers, musicians, people who simply stood with others as a friend. All these wielding different gifts, yet all also with the same beautiful and powerful love of Christ within them.

Paul says this to the elders of Ephesus in Acts:

> Therefore take heed to yourselves and to all the flock, among which the Holy Spirit has made you overseers, to shepherd the church of God which He purchased with His own blood. (Acts chapter 20, verse 28 NKJV)

People talk about being inward versus outward looking. The church, built from ordinary people, also carries a divine power as these Spirit-filled individuals allow God to reveal opportunities to bless in the everyday. Together, the church is a team, directed by Christ, reaching out arms that heal, protect and love.

The effect

> Therefore I remind you to stir up the gift of God which is in you through the laying on of my hands. For God has not given us a spirit of fear, but of power and of love and of a sound mind. (2 Timothy chapter 1, verses 6-7 NKJV)

The possibilities are endless when we choose to trust God. He gives us the ability not only to conquer our own fears and challenges, but also to help others conquer theirs. The power we have been given in Christ does not glorify ourselves, but glorifies God as it reveals His perfect love and His power over even the grave. What can stand against our God?

As for us, we have a responsibility that comes with knowing the power of God in our lives. The gift of grace God gave us was never meant to be selfishly hoarded, but to be shared with as many people as would receive it. The spiritual gifts given to us were never meant to lay dormant, but to be fanned into flames so that we might experience freedom and victory in life with Christ and share this with others.

This ultimate superpower, faith, is itself a gift from God and its effect is far-reaching. We can all know power in the Name of Jesus, so let us cry out to Him and give Him glory.

JANE EYRE AND THE QUESTION: IS THERE SUCH A THING AS 'THE ONE'?

by Rebecca Moore

There seems to be a belief today that the idea of there being a person created to be your other half doesn't exist: "There are many people out there suited to you and you just have to choose one that you like". While this may be true and work for many people, I certainly don't want to 'throw the baby out with the bath water' as the saying goes.

Watching the movie Jane Eyre recently, I was moved again at the strength of the power of love in the story. I had read the book many years ago, but the reminder of the story showed me just how far we, as a society, have drifted away from the idea that our God is big enough to create and predestine us to meet our soulmate and so become 'one'.

Jane Eyre—a quick run-down

Here is a quick run-down of the story, and I mean quick because it is a very long book! The main points: Jane's parents die and leave her to the care of relatives who reject her and put her in a girl's home. She has a very difficult life growing up and eventually finds employment as a governess at Mr Rochester's estate. Despite her poor position in life, and Mr Rochester's pick of wealthy beautiful women, the two have a heart connection which cannot be denied.

> I sometimes have a queer feeling with regard to you – especially when you are near me, as now: it is as if I had a string somewhere under my left ribs, tightly and inextricably knotted to a similar string situated in the corresponding quarter of your little frame. And if that boisterous channel, and two hundred miles or so of land some broad between us, I am afraid that cord of communion will be snapt; and then I've a nervous notion I should take to bleeding inwardly. —Charlotte Bronte, Jane Eyre (Mr Rochester)

Jane is driven away through unfortunate events and finds employment elsewhere but suffers greatly at the separation. On realising where her heart belongs, she travels back to the estate, only to find a great fire has occurred and Mr Rochester is now blind. Without saying anything (as the movie shows), she approaches him as he sits bereft by a tree, his heart recognises her presence and they declare their love for each other. The two are together again, as two complete souls.

Life is stranger than fiction

I know this is a 'soppy love story', but real life is often stranger than fiction. When I was 15, I went to a Bible camp. By the time I came home, I knew that my soul had met its soulmate, and I told my mum that I had met the man I was going to marry. We married three years later.

I have friends and relatives that have had similar experiences, living opposite sides of the country and meeting in one place and 'knowing'. Others have realised later into their friendships or courting, but still had the unmistakable 'knowing' that this was 'the one'.

For some, everything on their list of things to look for in a spouse was ticked, but the heart connection confirmed it.

Many stories happened in the most unlikely of places.

Have we as a society lost the wonder and amazement of God's creation of romance and two souls becoming one? Years ago, when I was studying, we were told that words like 'soul' and 'spirit' were shunned in literature now, and not popular. But in doing this, have we allowed popular culture to dismiss the miracle of love?

Jesus says in Matthew chapter 19, verses 4-6:

> "Haven't you read," he replied, "that at the beginning the Creator 'made them male and female,' and said, 'For this reason a man will leave his father and mother and be united to his wife, and the two will become one flesh'? So, they are no longer two, but one flesh. Therefore, what God has joined together, let no one separate". (NIV)

Notice he says, "what God has joined together"?

Can we trust God with our future spouse?

If God knew us before we were born and predestined us, if He knew every day of our lives before even we stepped one out, if He knows every hair on our heads, then if we ask, believing that He holds our future in His hands, is He not able to bring 'the one' even from the most obscure place on the other side of the world, into the same space where our souls recognise each other and never again can be separate?

Even author Charlotte Bronte had her views on how great God is in the presence of romance:

> We know that God is everywhere; but certainly we feel His presence most when His works are on the grandest scale spread before us; and it is in the unclouded night-

sky, where His worlds wheel their silent course, that we read clearest His infinitude, His omnipotence, His omnipresence. (Charlotte Bronte, Jane Eyre)

Did not God create Adam and Eve to be together? Abraham and Sarah; Isaac and Rebekah; Jacob and Rachel; Boaz and Ruth; Elkanah and Hannah? These relationships were not without trouble but had eternal purpose. It is important to mention that if you are going to live your life with someone—and that could be a very long time together—you want to make sure it's the right someone. Life's trials will be easier to endure with 'the one' than someone that felt good at the time.

So, I say to the young people of today and to those who are looking for 'the one'— pray, pray, pray, and trust God to handle it. Then get on with things, because one day God might just surprise you when you least expect it.

THE UNCERTAINTIES OF A NEW YEAR

By Esther Koh

After four years of being a stay-at-home mum with my two boys, I'm once again heading back to university…or so I thought. Things don't always go as planned. Life is full of unexpected roadblocks and detours.

Unfortunately, although I gave my best and did well for the test and interview, I was not chosen for the limited entry programme I had applied for because I wasn't a match with any mentor.

This came as a very disappointing news, as it was something I was not only excited about but also necessary for me to realise my dream of teaching again. Ending this year full of uncertainties of the coming year didn't help any bit with coping with this disappointment.

With only a few weeks left before the year ends, and with my carefully thought out plan for the next year crumbling into pieces, I was left scrambling in uncertainties—uncertain of my career, my studies, my children's childcare plans—for my future.

As the new year steadily approaches, it feels so easy to fall into the cycle of fear and worry, both of which don't contribute in improving the situation at all. Either this or I could choose to face every challenge acknowledging that they are opportunities for me to rely on God to expand my capabilities and character.

After all, every challenge comes with its opportunities, if we could only recognise it.

Without the challenge

Many of us would prefer, though, for the opportunity to come without any challenge. If we could conveniently do away with the challenge, why not?

We want a high paying job without any challenging colleagues and superiors.

We want to score A's without challenging assignments and tests.

We want children without challenging behaviours and antics.

We want a relationship without challenging conversations and thoughts.

In short, it would be great if everything was smooth sailing without the challenges. Since challenges only seem to stress us out and leave us burnt out, it would be good to do without them.

However, we fail to see that missing a challenge is also akin to missing an opportunity.

Missing out on opportunities

When we choose to do things the easy way without a challenge, we miss out on opportunities—opportunities to rely on God; opportunities to grow.

We were not made to be independent of God. Rather to dwell in His presence and drawing on Him to be the best us. Without any challenge, we grow complacent and begin to trust our own abilities to handle things. Subsequently, we grow distant from God because He is unneeded.

While all might seem well, and we feel that we are excelling in life, there will constantly still be the insatiable feeling of needing more. This need can only be filled by coming to the one who created us, for only the Creator can reveal to us the purpose of our existence.

We might think that there's nothing wrong with not relying on God. However, this actually means that we miss the whole point of our existence—we were made to be in a relationship with God.

As Colossians chapter 1, verse 16 says, 'All things were created through Him and for Him'.

Without a challenge, we are essentially not growing. We are happy in our comfort zone. There is no need to stretch or go the extra mile as everything is working as planned. In other words, we are stagnant in our growth when, in all actuality, our DNA shouts growth.

Needing the challenges

If anything, we actually need challenges in our lives. Instead of praying for a life without challenges and hoping that God will rid our lives of them, we should pray for the wisdom and guidance to face each challenge that comes our way.

There's no testimony without a test, no message without a mess. Let's not skip the challenge, for the challenge is needed to make us ready for the opportunity that comes with it.

That way, we draw closer to God with every challenge and deepen our relationship with Him. As we know Him more, we know ourselves more too. The challenge is what grounds our faith in Him and builds our character with the experience needed for our upcoming task.

Facing the uncertainties with the certainties

Undoubtedly there will still be uncertainties, in fact the uncertainties will grow in number. However, the uncertainties are of the perishable things of this world, while what we gain are the certainties of eternity.

Though we don't know how much we will earn, we know of God's provision to provide for us.
Though we don't know what we should study, we know God is able to use anything we offer to Him.

Though we don't know what our day will be like, we know of God's strength to sustain us through it.

Each new year may be a year full of challenges with so many uncertainties. This time though, I'm not going to waste my time worrying about the uncertainties while wishing the challenges away. Instead, I'll cling tightly to the certainties of God to carry me through each of my wobbly steps.

INVOLUNTARY CELIBACY IN THE DIGITAL CHURCH

by Blake Gardiner

One summer youth camp, a friend commented to me, "I hope I don't have the gift of celibacy". I found his comment odd, illogical, unbiblical; yet I understood. I, too, had been troubled by the same notion as I found his comment echoed and resonated with a phenomenon increasingly prevalent, not only in our culture, but in our pews.

The coercive curse of celibacy

In other writings, I have raised the question whether contemporary church cultures promote healthy relationships. Digressing from this issue and drawing back the metaphorical onion lawyers further, I feel a common experience of many young adults is that of an intense expectation to marry.

Probing questions from parents, elders, our pastor, peers, and the rest of our congregations increase in frequency as we stack up our birthdays. The gift of celibacy dissipates and is replaced by a curse one feels we did not deserve but was beyond our control.

In justification of this mind-set, we find in 1 Corinthians chapter 7, verse 9, Paul's comments speaking of the unmarried and the widowed:

'But if they cannot exercise self-control, let them marry.

For it is better to marry than to burn with passion'. (NKJV)

All the while, we have forgotten Paul's commendation two verses earlier in 1 Corinthians chapter 7, verse 7: 'I wish that all were as I myself am'.

Speaking of his singleness, Paul concedes he wishes that all were as him. He later explains the reasoning for this stems from the undivided devotion to God a single life provides.

Yet, we too easily memorise Paul's comments in verse 9 and exclude his preceding comment in verse 7.

In the world, this sentiment has resulted in the 'incel' (involuntary celibacy) movement, infamous in recent years for being dominated by young males who have lashed out in anger for lack of a romantic or sexual relationship. While one would be stretched to find this behaviour in the church, the seeds are too easily set by our corporate behaviour.

The instantaneous irritation of Instagram

Before I am called out for my hypocrisy, yes, I am a young single male writing on the matter of involuntary celibacy. I write this, not out of frustration, but out of a feeling of brokenness not only for our churches, but for the predicament we are now in.

The rise of Instagram and the like has now painted an environment where a few seconds of scrolling through our newsfeed manipulates and exaggerates our emotions. We begin to drive ourselves deeper into comparisons. How many times do we toy with the perfect filter, the right lighting, the wittiest caption, or the profound hashtags? And in response, we read these posts. First, we laugh, comment, or 'heart' the post. Then we compare that which we do not have with what others already have, based on a single post.

We also know that we are often inclined that, once we feel a certain emotion, we will act in a way that will exacerbate its intensity. If I am feeling unsatisfied, I will seek to find that which I believe will satisfy me, and by extension I look for what others have that satisfies them. Instagram and social media create the perfect environment to feed this. The struggle with relationship, singleness, and loneliness is no exception to this.

The biblical counter-narrative

There is a plethora of articles on the issues of social media, this is not one of those. This is an attempt at a reminder of the counter-narrative we must continuously wrestle with.

This is a call to self-control as a fruit of the Spirit. The self-control to be content with the grace we have been given each day as we seek to honour God through our lives. In response, we must earnestly ask ourselves whether using social media as a platform for comparison honours God.

This is also a call for a more radical shift in our churches. It is not a novel call, it is another warning bell amongst many others. In the realm of relationships, discontentment, celibacy, and social media, we have a secular society which mirrors our own actions in many facets. In some fashion, they are almost identical in their treatment of this awkward young adult phase many of us experience and the continual questions of marriage.

This should scare us, but I don't think it does—for the simple reason that we are already too caught up in our own comparisons to realise that the only comparison that matters is where we sit before God and God alone.

JESUS KNOWS HOW THIS FEELS

by Cartia Moore

I feel so betrayed when my family eats the last block of chocolate in the house. Did they not think of me in those last few moments where they took that small little square of goodness and shoved it into their mouths?

I wish I had a Yoda voice that could creep into their heads when this happens. "Mother...eat the chocolate, you shall not", or "Fill your beds with dirt I shall do...", but alas, I am not that intellectually powerful.

Betrayal—oh, doesn't that word have a sonic boom sound to it, as it leaves your lips and rumbles through the air, ready to rebound off the wall and hit you right back in the face and, well, betray you. Typical. Should have seen that one coming.

Life is not without betrayal. We all go through it, whether it's from ourselves, our friends or family, expectations, our leaders, or in the simple things like something that you really just didn't expect cutting into your day and snatching up all the goodness.

In Luke chapter 17, verse 1, Jesus teaches His disciples:

> Betrayals are inevitable, but great devastation will come to the one guilty of betraying others. (TPT)

The 'friend'

As unwelcoming as it is, betrayals of all kinds are inevitable, since sin entered the world.

When friends betray us it hurts, but God understands what is going on and he can help us. It is a painful thing when it happens, because we trusted someone only to have them break that trust, but we have to remember that we have probably—whether intentionally or not—betrayed others too, and know how bad that makes us feel when we realise.

There is no real comfort in being betrayed, but the best thing we can do during those times is to focus our attention on the Living Word and let that be the source of comfort for us.

When we delve into the Bible, one of the most important events recorded actually helps us to open our eyes to the fact that, when we are betrayed, we are not alone. We are not the only ones who have been betrayed, others also go through it—even Jesus!

The betrayer

One of the biggest betrayals recorded in history happened in the lead up to Jesus' death. Jesus was betrayed by one of his own disciples; his friend, whom he loved very much.

Judas betrayed Jesus by turning him over to Pontius Pilate's soldiers. Whatever drove him to do it, you find yourself asking 'how on earth could he do that to Jesus?' You can just imagine how heartbroken Jesus would have been.

Because of Judas' betrayal of Jesus, Jesus died a horrific death on the cross. But, like always, this was all part of the plan and was allowed to happen in order for Jesus to save the world. He brought good out of the bad, and that is what he can do with us and our situations.

There are times in our lives when we may feel the pain of betrayal from a close friend. These moments certainly hurt and can leave us feeling heartbroken and upset. Sometimes we don't even know the cause as to why someone has betrayed us in the first place. We may be left feeling hurt because someone we once trusted has decided to turn on us, leaving us feeling alone and bewildered. But when we trust in Jesus, we can be overcomers, in Jesus name!

If Jesus was betrayed but still managed to overcome death, imagine what we can do with the power of our God living inside of us. Imagine how much stronger and more resilient we will become because we let God carry our betrayal instead of holding it close to our hearts wondering 'why did this happen'?

Grace

We don't have to face death, or the burden of carrying everyone's sin on our shoulders like Jesus did for us, but when people turn on us, we can actually receive this amazing quality called grace. It's up to us whether or not we choose to use it.

Jesus had ultimate grace when he was betrayed, persecuted, humiliated, and killed on that cross. While he looked upon all those who betrayed him, he turned to the Lord and said:

> "Father forgive them, for they do not know what they are doing" (Luke chapter 23, verse 34 NIV).

Forgiveness and grace from Jesus in a moment of pure agony—that is absolute selflessness. Even as he stared death in the face, he showed grace, as he heard the cry of the criminal next to him say,

> "Jesus, remember me when you come into your kingdom." Jesus answered him, "Truly I tell you, today you will be with me in paradise." (Luke chapter 23, verse 42-43 NIV)

Forgiveness

Jesus could have reacted towards all those who accused him, but instead he showed them love and grace by forgiving them. Forgiveness can cure not only our hearts in the situation of betrayal, but we get the opportunity to teach those who betray us, how we should be treated by showing them what they could not show us. Luke chapter 6, verse 31 says: "Do to others as you would have them do to you".

We need ask God for grace. I know it can be hard, but Jesus is with us. He led by example, now it is our turn to do the same. We need to graciously forgive those who hurt us, no matter what they did, so that we can be free of their mistakes and our heartache and turn our focus onto Jesus who will guide us into the wonderful future he has planned for us.

GRANNY GET YOUR GUN
by John Skinner

My maternal grandmother was a 'good ole girl,' much loved by her grandchildren. Taller than many of her vintage with lovely long hair and, while no longer the good looking young lass by the time I came along, she had the beauty of maturity. Being the oldest grandchild I had certain liberties with her, mostly, though, I had to take responsibility for anything the younger ones did.

When young, I spent many months on the farm between Armidale and Bundarra in the New England district of New South Wales. It was super-fine wool growing country where the family ran about 2,000 head of Merinos and about 100 Hereford cows. Their average wool micron size was 16-18, in other words, super-fine and suitable, in its day, for the finest Italian suits.

The family secret

Now Granny never lived in town until her last couple of years, she was a country girl from start to finish and had all the skills to go with it.

She came from a well-to-do family who were pioneers in the district and how she came to marry my less-than well-to-do grandfather was a family secret. The truth being, she became pregnant at 18, he was 28, the result being my mother and we were never supposed to know.

She taught me how to crack a whip, she taught me how to shoot snakes with the 'orchard gun' (.410 shotgun)—the farm had an over-abundance of Eastern Browns, the most deadly of common snakes in Australia—she taught me to ride with only a corn-bag for a saddle, she loaned me her horses (she had been an outstanding lady rider in her youth), and she made me learn to drink black tea from wine bottles when out in the paddock away from home.

Farm snakes

One abiding memory is of us kids searching through the farm sheds, under sheets of iron, or in the creek bed looking for snakes. They weren't hard to find.

As soon as we found one, the shout went out for Granny to bring the gun.

We'd stand back and the old girl, with her skirt hitched up and her long legs going '10 to the dozen', would come running from the house, loading the gun on the run and shooting the snake before she stopped. I've never seen a better shot on the run than my grandmother. She'd tell us to stay away from the old sheds but was no sooner out of sight than we were back on the search again.

I never felt more at home than when I'd help her light the kitchen fire at daybreak and make toast with a wire fork held in front of the coals before the men went out to milk the house cows. It was a farm which supported five families in those days and now barely supports my cousin with his family having left for town jobs.

Christian values

Later in life I spent many happy hours with Granny and was there toward the end when she passed away.

Granny had been brought up with Christian values; she'd attended church as a teenager and had been to many church functions with her family, as was fairly common in the early 20th century, until she married my grandfather. Unlike my paternal grandfather, a wonderful Christian man, my maternal grandfather was anything but.

So now I often wonder about my loving grandmother. Did she hold onto those Christian values to the end? Did she believe in Jesus as the Son of God? Had she been born again?

I also wonder if I should have asked her these questions before she died. I had the opportunity, I had the faith and desire, but I didn't. If she died an unbeliever, where does it leave me? I loved her so and yet I may have let her pass to the next world as an unbeliever and it challenges me to this day never to let it happen again.

DRAMA! WHO NEEDS IT?

by Rebecca Moore

A cyclone was due to hit my town recently and there was a little bit of nervous excitement in the air. People stocked up on food, cancelled weekend events and prepared for bad weather. News reports kept us up to date on what we could expect in the coming days and preparations were made.

We awoke Saturday morning to a beautiful sun-shiny day. The sky was clear and blue and, really, you couldn't ask for better weather. My husband and I even had breakfast by the beach—just gorgeous!

The cyclone had been downgraded overnight and the only effects we could see from it came in the form of some awesome (yet dangerous) surf which our local surfers enjoyed, drawing crowds of local onlookers to the beach.

Deflated

I'm not sure, but I kind of feel that our town was a little bit deflated at the lack of action from the cyclone. Radio talk-show hosts talked about the fizzle-out of the cyclone and some even offered to give a shout-out to those organisations who had cancelled events for the weekend—and then life went back to normal.

It amused me a little. While the drama of the impending

cyclone put everyone on alert, the rise in adrenaline had many looking forward to it—even if just a little. On reflection, I'm really glad that the cyclone didn't hit our town as I would be devasted to see this beautiful part of the world torn up by extreme weather.

Drama attracts drama

It's a little like life really. The whiff of drama often attracts drama. People are attracted to it because it is something out of the ordinary that takes the attention off oneself while casting it on to others. Gossip magazines thrive on the drama in celebrity lives and if there is not enough to report, they'll make it up.

In reality though, blessings lay in the lack of drama. To live a consistent life without unnecessary overly dramatized situations is a much preferred, uncomplicated way to live.

Paul talks about this in chapter four of his first letter to the Thessalonians:

> Yet we urge you, brothers and sisters…to make it your ambition to lead a quiet life: You should mind your own business and work with your hands, just as we told you, so that your daily life may win the respect of outsiders and so that you will not be dependent on anybody.
> (verses 9-12)

While I secretly enjoy a little drama in the out-of-the-ordinary surprises that often occur in my life (so long as they aren't detrimental to anyone's health or well-being), there is enough that happens naturally to prevent me from wanting to encourage any of it. When you think about it, God wants to lead us beside quiet waters not beside tidal waves! He doesn't antagonise storms, he calms them.

> He makes me lie down in green pastures, he leads me beside quiet waters, he refreshes my soul. He guides me along the right paths for his name's sake. (Psalm chapter 23, verses 2-3 NIV)

So, when the threat of unwanted drama looms before me, the quicker it is diffused, the better. God wants us to live a life that is free of unnecessary complications and to do all that we can to live at peace with each other.

> Be completely humble and gentle; be patient, bearing with one another in love. Make every effort to keep the unity of the Spirit through the bond of peace. There is one body and one Spirit, just as you were called to one hope when you were called; one Lord, one faith, one baptism; one God and Father of all, who is over all and through all and in all. (Ephesians chapter 4, verses 2-6 NIV)

A FAITH BOOST
by Manuele Teofilo

When you think you know and have a reasonable understanding of God's love, He shows you His love in a much deeper way. I have experienced His love several times in my walk with Christ. Over New Year's, I was reminded of how much God loves and my faith got a boost.

The young adults of my local church in Manukau went on a beach mission in Tairua over New Year's. I put my name down to go on the trip, but it took a while to work out the logistics.

I had to find someone to help me with personal needs and find transport. The team that organized the trip generously included working out the logistics of taking me to Tairua in their planning efforts.

I asked my mum, the most loving and giving person I know, to come with me. Even though she wasn't feeling the best, she agreed to support me in Tairua.

To resolve the transport and accommodation issues I tried to find a place for my family to rent. This way my family could drive me to Tairua and I would stay with them. However, I couldn't find a place that was affordable or accessible.

People on the beach mission team were either staying in tents or homes which is impractical for me. So, the organizers also had to figure out a suitable accommodation for my mum and me. Eventually, a week before the trip the people hosting us in Tairua found a solution.

I was hopeful that I was going to be able to make the trip because my support person and accommodation was sorted. At the same time, I was unsure if I was going, because we were still trying to work out how to get me and my wheelchair to Tairua. My only idea was to ask my dad a huge favour.

I need a miracle!

The week leading up to the trip was really challenging. I was asking God for reassurance that He wanted me to go on the trip. Despite the transport issue deep down God gave me a strong sense that somehow, I was going to Tairua.

I just thought it was a crazy idea to ask my dad to drive almost two hours just to drop us off and drive back, then again to pick us up.

I was hesitant to ask my dad because I thought he might think that I was out of my mind and say no. Dad wasn't impressed when mum and I presented the idea. He didn't give a clear yes or no straight away. With two days before we went down to Tairua I still didn't know how I was going.

I messaged the pastor leading the trip saying that I felt so much was against me. Just two days out and mum was feeling unwell and dad hadn't said yes yet. However, I felt a strong sense to not give up. So, we prayed for a way to open up.

The very next morning I woke up hearing dad say he's driving to Tairua over the phone to someone. Mum came into my room looking better, asking if I still wanted to go.

Everything turned around that morning and God couldn't have said "you're going!" any louder.

Beach mission trip

The fact that God got a guy with high needs to a mission trip was only the start of my faith boost. Over four days we witnessed people in our team and people in Tairua get healed when we prayed for them. Everyone on the team was happy for the people who got healed and all grew in our faith.

Before the trip we prayed and ask for clues (words of knowledge) to find treasures (people) that we can pray for, encourage and share the Gospel to. My clue was a guy with a green top. It took a while for many of us to find our treasures.

However, when we eventually spotted our treasures it was a challenge for us to step out in faith and go talk to the person. Speaking to our treasures we all saw why God led us to them. My friend and I got to pray and encourage a guy who was feeling anxious about starting his new job as a school teacher.

I have talked about my challenges of getting to the beach mission trip. However, everyone that went on the beach mission trip had their own challenges. God showing His love through our friends (and family) helped each person to push through the challenges.

Let me take care of it God says

I learnt so many things going on the beach mission and particularly about God's love. As I reflected on the trip the biggest thing I learnt was that God took care of everything. Realizing this got me excited for this year because He will continue to do great things for me.

A DUTY OF CARE

by Jessica Knell

Our fragmented world desperately cries out for mercy—while we feebly attempt to shelter our minds from acknowledging the brokenness, remaining ignorant to others suffering in conflict-stricken nations or those who are trapped in cycles of poverty.

Our conversations lack vulnerability as we steer away from addressing how we truly are going. We shift uncomfortably away from addressing battles with mental health, abuse or pornography.

In the comfort of our self-made caverns, we refute our duty of care to each other.

We are a broken, desperate and unholy people. Yet, God hears our cry, delivers mercy, and refuses to pass us by.

The Good Samaritan

> Love the Lord your God with all your heart and with all your soul and with all your strength and with all your mind; and, love your neighbour as yourself. (Luke chapter 10, verse 27 NIV)

In Luke chapter 10, verses 25-37 Jesus shares the parable of the Good Samaritan. An expert of the law challenges Jesus about the prerequisites to inheriting eternal life.

Through a process of Socratic questioning, Jesus reveals the man's motives and compels us to consider if we truly love our neighbours.

Motives of the heart

> But he wanted to justify himself, so he asked Jesus, "And who is my neighbour"? (Luke chapter 10, verse 29 NIV)

Essentially the expert of the law asked Jesus, "what is the minimum I can do to check this box," and "exactly who is worthy of love?"

This question is not coming from the outflowing of an eager-to-please heart. In contrast, his motives are selfish, focusing on the minimum amount of effort required to get a free pass into heaven.

This misguided question could easily be coming from any of us.

We excuse ourselves from loving others. We continue to ask the Lord which people deserve to be loved. We refuse to allow our hearts to be softened as we persistently pursue what is comfortable.

Passing to the other side

The dying man lay naked and alone. Desperate, afraid, and vulnerable.

Yet both the Priest and the Levite refuse to step into the uncomfortable. They relinquish their duty of care to the dying man. Instead, they elect to pass to the other side of the road making the intentional effort to ignore his dying plea.

In contrast, the Samaritans were a marginalised people in society. This could have easily hardened the Samaritan's heart towards helping others. However, the Samaritan stepped into the uncomfortable. He acknowledged his duty of care to his fellow man in an act of outrageous mercy.

Mercy has the ability to break down walls. It transcends differences in culture, gender, socioeconomic status, and all man-made societal divides. Mercy acknowledges our humanness, our need for compassion and forgiveness.

God has instructed us to love, and in doing so we are called to step into the uncomfortable.

Loving our neighbours

> And what does the Lord require of you? To act justly and to love mercy and to walk humbly with your God. (Micah chapter 6, verse 8 NIV)

In Luke chapter 10, verse 37, Jesus concludes the parable of the Good Samaritan by challenging the expert of the law to go and do likewise. This is not a passive instruction, rather it is a challenge to act out mercy.

So what does it look like for us to live a life of mercy today?

I suggest that it starts with a willing heart. A willingness to be inconvenienced and readjust our priorities in order to accommodate the needs of others. Furthermore, it requires us to look for opportunities along our daily journeys to promote equality and demonstrate compassion and forgiveness.

Although it may be uncomfortable, we are challenged to love our neighbours regardless. A simple instruction, but difficult to obey. Do we truly love our neighbours?

We are not alone

Paul, in Romans chapter 7, verse 19, explains his inner conflict of wanting to do what is right but continually doing wrong.

However, we know that we love because Christ first loved us, and we can be assured that in knowing Christ we are changed beings. We do not need to depend on our own strength to earn enough points to gain entry into heaven. Jesus has already paid the price for our salvation.

Although our own will fails us, God's character is love and He will never pass us by.

Section 4

Culturality

REDEEMING CULTURE

by Jesse Moore

If you've ever tried to build a sandcastle in the middle of a hurricane then you're pretty weird, but you would also know exactly what it feels like to be disheartened by modern culture. Often the incremental steps taken by Christians to change culture and politics can be completely overhauled by secularity and contemporary values; it seems that every step forward we take ends up being five steps backwards.

Judging by passionate posts on social media, young people seem to care more about the perceived possibility of climate change than they do about the certainty of thousands of unborn children dying from abortion laws. Political parties benefit from the uneducated, all the while universities can make special bursaries of well over a grand exclusively for students that identify as LGBTI+. Finally, a professional rugby player can be kicked out of his league and publicly vilified for voicing his beliefs—and this is just in one month.

While this is sad and disappointing, the downward spiral of culture and hegemonic views is nothing new and isn't the end of the world. This has been happening since the beginning of time and is addressed relentlessly in the Bible, in fact it's the very premise to most stories and teachings in the book. The challenges don't date and are completely relevant now, as they were back then.

Wilberforce

A great example of strength in the face of adversity is the well-known William Wilberforce, the poster-boy and key figure in the abolition of slavery. Wilberforce was a social reformer who dedicated his life to ending the slave trade by presenting facts, arguments, and evidence before the House of Commons, which was often futile.

Friend and mentor, John Newton, a former slave ship captain who wrote the hymn Amazing Grace, quoted the story of Daniel and the lion's den to Wilberforce, suggesting that Daniel was also a public figure who faced adversity but kept his faith in the Lord that none of his enemies could prevail. Newton said to Wilberforce "the God whom you serve continually is able to preserve and deliver you, he will see you through".

After facing adversity, physical attacks, declining health, and his reputation dragged through the mud, saying that Wilberforce didn't want to run at some point, I believe, would be completely inaccurate. To reject the money-making machine that slavery was to the British at this time, and support its abolition, required commitment beyond time, money, and status, as this was a cultural shift he fought for—not just a political one.

Bonhoeffer

I often write about Dietrich Bonhoeffer, but that's because the book by Eric Metaxas is so long you want to use that information regularly to justify the investment of time. Nevertheless, he's a brilliant example of someone who, against the odds, defends righteousness and doesn't back down from the fight.

In the early 1930's, a few years before the Nazi party gained power, a young pastor clued onto the party's true intentions—which were clear to anyone who looked. Regardless, church leaders of Germany turned a blind eye to this threat.

Even after the sending of letters to fellow pastors and leveraging radio air-time to expose Nazi lies, the church of Germany didn't just submit to Nazi power but endorsed it, supporting the implementation of Nazi values in the German church—now deceptively named 'The German Christians'.

With the pastors of Germany siding with a Fuhrer instead of God, Bonhoeffer was faced with only three options. The first one was ignoring the problem or running away (granted, this wasn't the worst idea considering he was up against an empire fuelled by hate), deceiving the church, and turning a blind eye murdering millions of people. Secondly, he could have sided with them, "if you can't beat them, join them", and added to the problem.

But the third option, after his freedom to preach and write came to an abrupt end, realising he was of no use on the outside, Bonhoeffer joined the military intelligence agency where he was able to continue preaching and secretly work with the conspiracy against Hitler.

Bonhoeffer and Wilberforce both were able to elicit change and shift power by running head-on towards the problem instead of running away from it. Neither of these men could have served or found their purpose if they secluded themselves from a society of falling values.

Today, we are faced with different issues but the same challenge: will we stand up for righteousness and defend our freedoms by running head-first into the problem—or run from it?

A POLITICAL OR APOLITICAL GOD

by Roydon Ng

Jesus rode a donkey, so does that mean He's a Democrat or socialist? Jesus taught using the Parable of the Talents, so is He a capitalist? Let's take the elephant out of the room (so out goes 'Republican Jesus', too) and look at why Christians ought to steer clear of the partisan 'left vs right' divide.

Jesus did not endorse any economic or political system at all, so that's the first way we know he wasn't socialist. In fact, John chapter 18, verse 36 records Jesus as saying, "My kingdom is not of this world… my kingdom is from another place". He never said anything about any kind of government system or economic system which means that he wasn't a socialist—but he wasn't a capitalist either.

God's rule above human politics

It's quite clear that Jesus' ministry has never been about human governments. Jesus isn't a political or military revolutionary as many Jews had hoped or expected, which explains why many were disbelieving when he died on the Cross.

They expected Jesus to come in and be a political revolutionary and he wasn't that, and now we have 2000 years of Christianity. Again, going back to John chapter 18 verse 36, Jesus says:

> "My kingdom is not of this world. If it were, my servants would fight to prevent my arrest by the Jewish leaders. But now my kingdom is from another place". (NIV)

If you study political science or listen to many commentators, you'll often hear that the premise of establishing a system of governance is anarchy. Anarchy ranges from the mere existence of conservative voices to actual civil unrest and violence. Both socialism and capitalism are examples of human political systems invented in an unsuccessful attempt to fix the anarchy caused by the original sin of humanity's rebellion against God.

When humanity chose to run life our own way without God, we chose to put our trust in political systems. But choosing to live under God's rule means to put Jesus above human politics and live as a follower of Jesus. Which way will you choose to live?

As Matthew chapter 7, verses 16 to 20 tells us,

> By their fruit you will recognize them. Do people pick grapes from thornbushes, or figs from thistles? Likewise, every good tree bears good fruit, but a bad tree bears bad fruit. A good tree cannot bear bad fruit, and a bad tree cannot bear good fruit. Every tree that does not bear good fruit is cut down and thrown into the fire. Thus, by their fruit you will recognize them. (NIV)

Let's look at the fruits of this particular fig tree, human political systems, and we'll find that we've got over 100 million people since the beginning of the 20th century who have been killed by communism and socialism.

The Holocaust in World War II was bad, with six million

Jews murdered, but the deaths caused by the Soviet Union under Joseph Stalin and by Communist China under Mao Zedong have exceeded this. Stalin is estimated to have caused the death of 40–62 million people and Mao caused the death of 45–75 million people. Both the Nazis and the Communists placed belief in their leaders instead of God as supreme, and the results have been disastrous.

The reason behind Jesus' actions, such as helping the poor and healing the sick, isn't because Jesus believed in free healthcare as part of the His socialist economic policy. Nor did Jesus sell His services to the highest bidder or the most established in society. Jesus welcomed the children and healed those who could never repay, so He indeed wasn't an advocate of the profit-driven healthcare system either.

The everlasting kingdom

Also, all earthly kingdoms will ultimately fall, and the only good kingdom is God's kingdom. The Soviet Union was propagandised as the 'Worker's Paradise', but that collapsed in 1991. And even in the closer decades, there's clear evidence of failing countries even in Europe.

The economic crisis in Greece is just the start, and no matter how angry people may get when their entitlements are threatened or taken away, you can't create taxable income out of nowhere. And once the promises of welfare and government subsidies are cut because of austerity measures, the political support base will wither away and likely lead to violent civil unrest.

But it is only God's kingdom that will last forever and not face temporal challenges of budget cuts and unemployment. Psalm 145 verse 13 reminds us that God's

...kingdom is an everlasting kingdom, and your dominion endures through all generations. The LORD is trustworthy in all he promises and faithful in all he does. (NIV)

Both left wing, right wing, and every human political/economic system is sinful ideology as seen by its godlessness. The foundational element of socialism and communism is that man can do anything. Likewise, with capitalism and right-wing systems, it's all about self-pleasure through the accumulation of wealth.

All systems are merely human inventions that try to fix and reshape the world without acknowledging that it can be, and has only been, done through our risen Lord Jesus Christ.

We can rest assured that God's kingdom is one of everlasting life that welcomes all people who call upon Jesus to be Lord and Saviour. Whether your 'Vote 1' is for left- or right-wing candidates, what's most important is that you have Jesus as Number 1 in your life. All the promises from human politics will fade away, but it is only Jesus' relentless love that preserves and can heal humanity from the destruction caused by anarchy—the rejection of God.

JESUS DIDN'T TAP OUT
by Jeremy Dover

Sports chaplaincy has inspired many ministries. This story is one of SCA providing a model for a way to bring glory to God through sport.

The warehouse in Melbourne is surrounded by factories and government housing blocks. It is not the place you would expect to find a gym with a banner proclaiming "Jesus didn't tap".

The Brazilian Jiu Jitsu (BJJ) and Mixed Martial Arts (MMA) Fitness Centre, 'Renegade', is a great example of sport at its God-designed best. Sport brings people together and provides a lens for insight into life's deeper meaning. This story is about a gym that does both. It will inspire and challenge you to do the same in whatever area your chaplaincy or church is at.

Meeting place

Renegade is a meeting place for the local community. People from all walks of life come together to train at this centre. From the Anglican Theological College students, to the sports chaplains trying to keep up their fitness, to the local Muslims living in the housing commission flats, Renegade is a focal point for community. Sport brings people together and builds relationships beyond traditional boundaries. Renegade is an example of the way sport unites all regardless of culture or creed.

The bodily temple

If the body is often described as a temple then this gym is a place of worship. Renegade is a gym faithful to building strong bodies. Grappling requires explosiveness and power. Dedicated athletes refine technique and fitness over many hours of training. Sport teaches commitment and Renegade is an example of a centre training stronger bodies.

The REAL temple

This gym represents more than these concepts. God designed sport for our benefit and for His glory. When we participate in sport it reflects these God-designed attributes. In John chapter 1, Jesus is described as the Word of God that came and "dwelt among us". The term comes from the word tabernacle, which was the meeting place between the ancient Hebrew people and God. The community would gather around the tabernacle for corporate worship.

In many ways, Renegade has a similar aspect of both a physical meeting place, a place to train our earthly bodies, as well as an opportunity to worship the God that saves.

The true Temple/Tabernacle is Jesus. Through Him people come to find a true fitness. This is what Renegade offers. It points to Jesus through their Bible studies, conversations, prayers for its members and offering practical helps to those in need or the injured.

Tap out

In wrestling, the aim is to try and bring your opponent to a position of submission. You search for a point of weakness in which they 'tap out'. That is, they tap the mat as a sign they have submitted to the pain and acknowledge the superior strategy of their opponent. At this point, the bout is lost.

But Jesus didn't tap. Even as Jesus faced the wrath of God and judgement for the sins of the world, Jesus did not submit to temptation and evade this sacrifice. He conquered sin and death and won the victory through His resurrection. Renegade gym points to this Good News through a banner that explains 'Jesus didn't tap'.

Sport is more than just building bodies. It is about relationships. God uses sport to build these relationships and Renegade is a great example of the ways all these aspects come together for His glory. It truly is a remarkable centre that shines such a light into its local area.

LOVE, MORE THAN A FEELING

by Matthew Thornton

It goes without saying that globalisation and social media have changed the world as we know it.

The world has become a marketplace, and everyday we are bombarded with advertisements and promotions. It seems as if everything revolves around making the next buck.

We have more choices and more options than any other time in human history. If there is something we want, chances are some company, somewhere in the world, can provide it for us. More than that, if a company's product does not completely satisfy our needs, we won't hesitate to find an alternative.

In this consumerist culture, getting what we want, when we want it and how we want it is no longer a hope, but an expectation. An expectation that breeds selfishness and entitlement.

Social media is no help either. Algorithms are designed that you only see the content you're interested in. Your opinion, your interests are elevated and everything else is but an echo chamber.

Slowly but surely, a world bounded only by your interests is formed and we start to believe that the rest of the world should revolve around our happiness and satisfaction too.

A counterfeit love

I worry that consumerism, self-centeredness, and entitlement have degraded our relationships, and contaminated the way we view love itself.

Our view of love has become transactional. If we like a person, if a person conjures up that emotion of 'love' within us, we respond with loving actions. If someone doesn't evoke this feeling, we simply look for other 'alternatives'. Love has been reduced to a response, a reaction to a feeling.

> More relationships have failed because too many view love selfishly. [...]. Love isn't self-serving. Nor is it an emotion. The choice to act and respond through love will, at times, go directly against what you're feeling. (Restored Prodigal)

To love without liking

I don't know about you, but for a long time the commandment "love your enemies" (Matthew chapter 5, verse 44) frustrated and discouraged me. I couldn't work out how I was supposed to 'love' my enemy if I didn't 'like' them. I thought that it wasn't really 'love' if the characteristic emotion wasn't felt with it.

But surely the truest form of love is when we choose to show it even when we don't feel or desire it?

There are things that people may do that are evil, sinful, or even just annoying. But when these act as a barrier to loving people, we prevent the incredible transformation that can occur.

In every human heart, I think there is a longing to be fully known and fully loved. A desire to know that, despite what has been done in the past, or will be done in the future, that there is something in that person that is cherished and deserving of love.

The Greek word for love in Matthew chapter 5 verse 44 is defined as a "discriminating affection that involves choice and selection".

So, when we see the sin, the evil, the annoyance, and choose to act as if we love them anyway, we really are 'loving' our neighbour. Arguably, we are showing love in its most beautiful form.

> Love in this second sense isn't merely a feeling. It is a deep unity, maintained by will and deliberately strengthen by habit. (Mere Christianity, C.S. Lewis)

Choosing an unreactive love

I think the Kingdom love is more than just feelings. It is rooted in choice and is deeper and far more encompassing than the reactive love we are sold in this world.

> To love your neighbour is to see your neighbour. To see somebody, really to see somebody, you have to love somebody. (The Remarkable Ordinary, Frederick Buechner)

It is the type of that love unburdens shame and pretence. When people no longer feel that they have to 'perform' to receive our love, they are truly free to find themselves, to discover all He has made them to be.

It cultivates unity, breeds commitment and has the potential to bring heaven that much closer to earth. And it will change us too:

> The worldly man treats certain people kindly because he 'likes' them: the Christian, trying to treat everyone kindly, finds himself liking more and more people as he goes on—including people he could not even have imagined himself liking at the beginning. (Mere Christianity, C.S. Lewis)

Let's show love to others in spite of their actions towards us and, most importantly, in spite of our 'feelings' towards them—unconditionally in the truest sense.

Let's love, even when we don't 'like', and let's love by choice, not by response.

TRUST THE PROCESS
by Elise Pappas

I first heard these three words when we were going through our first and only round of in vitro fertilisation (IVF). Naturally, I was feeling anxious, overwhelmed and somewhat emotionally exhausted with the amount of medication to take and injections to administer.

We were about half way through the process when someone close to me encouraged me to trust the process. Here we were doing all we possibly could to have another child when someone suddenly stopped me, and reminded me that now I just need to trust the process.

This meant that I needed to trust that our infertility specialist with his 40 plus years of experience knew what he was doing, that he had a detailed plan laid out just for us. I also needed to trust my body that it too would do exactly as it should in response to all that was taking place. Then, of course, I needed to trust God, that He would do exactly as He said He would and deliver on His promise…whether that be in this way or another.

Trusting in the process isn't always easy. It's admitting that we are mere humans but that we have a powerful, almighty God who knows more, and can see further, than we can. It's being okay with the here and now, yet being unsettled enough to believe God for more. It's trusting that God can, and will, use anything to achieve His ultimate purpose, and to know that when we do all we can, then He steps in and does the rest.

Faith in action

In life we have to trust the process, that—even better than an infertility specialist having a plan for us—our God has the greatest plan for our family.

Our son loves to know where we are going when driving. He loves being able to watch the map in the car and follow the little blue arrow to see where we are in proportion to where we are headed.

Many of us are like this, we are content/happy when we can see how it's all going to play out. We are okay with the here and now when we can see what's going to happen a little further down the track. Unfortunately, we don't always know, nor can predict, the twists and turns that lie ahead but this is what faith is all about.

Long Play Concept

I recently heard a preacher talk about the 'long play concept': That we mustn't just be excited about the here and now but be excited to be in this faith journey for the long haul.

Like a farmer who plants seed knowing that it may be years before he reaps a harvest, we too must embrace the here and now and trust that God will use everything for His purpose. That those deepest desires and dreams we all have will come to be if we just stay the path and don't give up!

Pontius Pilate was the man who convicted Jesus of treason and ordered that He be crucified. Jesus's crucifixion was a part of God's plan for Jesus becoming the Saviour of the world. Pontius Pilate was a part of the process, a very important one. I believe Jesus knew and trusted that this too was a part of the greater process. I'm sure it didn't come without doubts or questions.

As we choose to trust the process, we too must remind ourselves and those around us that He's got it, to not quit or give up, to stop looking around, and that we are exactly where we are meant to be.

SHOULD I GIVE UP BEING A DAD?

by Russell Modlin

It can be tough being a Dad.
It can be tough being a Dad to three sons.

But spare a thought for the Melbourne father who recently was photographed at the Westfield Knox shopping centre in Melbourne's east. This photo was subsequently shared on Facebook with a status branding him a 'creep'. The mother's post was shared thousands of times and the father of three was forced to contact police to explain he was only taking a 'selfie' in front of a Darth Vader cut out sign to send to his children.

Granted: She has now apologised.
Granted: Many of the 20,000 people who shared the post have also apologised.

But what has this particular incident done to the reputation of fathers and men in the community?

Is every male a potential 'creep' or paedophile and about to harm your children? Are there any males you can trust with your children?

Can the male teacher at your child's school be trusted?

I spent a good hour on the Internet when this news story first broke to try and make sure this was story was valid and not some cruel hoax or joke. Sadly, this was not the case.

To give you the full story, the father of three said, "As I was walking out of Target I saw a very large Darth Vader cut out for taking photographs—it said 'May the 4th be with you'—and I've got three children and they love all that Comic-Con, Supanova, science fiction stuff".

The man said he took a quick selfie and saw a number of kids sitting down nearby and lining up to get their photo taken.

'I said "I'll only be a second, I'm taking a selfie to send to my kids". There was no parent present.'

'I then started walking out of the shop and was trying to work out how to send the photo to my three children.'

'Obviously as I was going out this woman has stalked me and taken a photo of me.'

The next day he was in a business meeting when he received a panicked call from his partner.

'My partner rang me and said she'd been contacted by somebody interstate who had seen the post and recognised me,' he said.

'Then she explained it to me and I was just flabbergasted at this stage that my photo is on Facebook with an allegation I've been speaking to children and taking children's photos.'

He said he immediately drove to Knox Police Station to identify himself.

'The police spoke to me at length in relation to the issue and my phone was analysed,' he said.

The woman's original Facebook post about the incident read: "Ok people, take a look at this creep".

She claimed the man approached her children while they were sitting watching Frozen on a screen in the children's clothing section at Target.

'He said, "hey kids", they looked up and he took a photo, then he said, "I'm sending this to a 16 yr old"', she wrote on Facebook.

The woman said she took a photo of the man then removed her children from the area and informed security.

'Centre management were straight onto and so are the police, hopefully he is caught [sic],' she wrote.

'Police said if he is a registered sex offender he will be charged, this happened at Knox, be safe with your kids.' (Source: DailyMail Australia)

I came home that night questioning my role as a father of three sons. Three sons who need their father to be the best example of a man they could ever see or live with. Three sons who need their father to be confident in his ability to raise them into the men God has called them to be. Three sons who need their father to unconditionally love his wife, to support her, to be there for her and encourage her to reach her potential.

Three sons who need the unconditional love of their Dad.

I went to school the next day beginning to question my role

as a Year Level Coordinator of ninety Year 9 students, both males and females. Does your child's school have many male teachers? I wonder if you have ever questioned why this might not be the case. I had a female colleague remark to me she had visited a local high school and there was one (1) male teacher amongst the teaching staff.

For too long years of abuse and neglect were ignored by church and government agencies, and The Royal Commission into Institutional Responses to Child Sexual Abuse was told every day of the 'creeps' and paedophiles who preyed on vulnerable children and the years of torment the victims have now endured.

Can we stop the distrust of men in the community?

It is up to fathers, it is up to men, to face up to their responsibilities of being a man and show the community we will no longer be objects of distrust. We need women to feel safe around us in our workplace. We need women to feel safe around us when we go out at night. We need our women to feel safe around us when we are at home.

My football team have supported the 'One punch can kill campaign' after losing two footballing fathers to senseless violence on our streets on the Sunshine Coast.

I have stood years ago arm and arm with my Aboriginal brothers in Alice Springs as they took a stand against violence in the community.

There are very good men out there. I know you know of at least one. Maybe send him a message. Could you post a positive message about him on social media? Write a note to your child's male teacher and tell him what a good job he is doing.

I don't want to feel guilty when a kid a school calls me their 'school Dad'. I don't want to feel guilty when I lovingly put my arms around my son in the shopping centre to embarrass them! I don't want to feel guilty when my sons give me a kiss goodnight. I don't want to feel guilty when a student is grieving over loss in their life and they need a pat on the back or want to give a hug, card or present at the end of the school year to say, "thanks, sir".

I don't want men to give up.

IN THE MIDDLE?
by David Goodwin

I was chatting with a Christian friend about the way in which our various social circles in life intersect, and I confessed that there are times I feel out of place in all of them. It made me think of one of my favourite Paul Colman Trio songs, 'In The Middle', which has the lines:

> Sometimes I feel like I'm in the middle
> Not safe enough for you
> Not crazy enough for some

Connections and Contradictions

I consider myself to be blessed to have a wide range of friends, people from all sorts of backgrounds, with all sorts of ideologies. One day I might be spending time with Christian friends, who share my faith and with whom I can discuss my beliefs. But, in the writing circles I move in—which are generally concerned with speculative fiction—the majority of people would best be described as secular humanists. A lot of my country friends have more conservative politics, while I have another group of friends who are far further to the left than I am.

Obviously, the reason I spend time with each of these groups is because I have something in common with them. But, sometimes a belief or position that is in sync with one group is completely at odds with one of the others, and that can cause a feeling of disconnect. However, over the past few years, I have come to realise that this is more of a blessing than a curse.

The Echosphere

One of the common elements I see across all these groups is that we tend to create a bubble of like minded opinions around ourselves. I have long abhorred this tendency in Christian circles—you can listen to Christian radio, watch Christian TV, find movies made for a Christian audience, and avoid the inconvenience of ever having your opinions or values challenged. Never mind that a part of your faith is about actually getting out there and being an influence the world.

But, this is certainly not limited to Christians. Both sides of politics have managed to create their own echospheres, with news outlets that reinforce their existing viewpoints, offering the ability to completely avoid anyone who disagrees with them. More and more, in every part of our life, we are able to filter the people we are exposed to.

Studies show that it has become a self-reinforcing cycle, with the most popular social media platform of them all, Facebook, actually deciding what you see in your timeline. The kind of posts that you regularly view or like will turn up more often, meaning you will see more of the things that tell you what you want to hear—giving you a slanted worldview.

The Cost of Comfort

This may not seem like a big deal, after all, who wants to be arguing all the time? But this mental comfort zone has a serious impact on the way we engage with the world. We are seeing an increasing degree of polarisation of worldviews, especially in the political arena. And, because we are so used to people agreeing with us we assume that people who disagree with us are stupid or, even worse, actively malevolent.

This unwillingness to believe that those on the other side of the fence might have arrived at their beliefs with the same care and consideration we did, has led to a world of 'us and them'. Bipartisanship has become a dirty word and finding common ground, or even a starting point for engagement, is becoming harder and harder.

This is equally as true with religion as with politics, but there is an added danger for Christians. Because we surround ourselves with those who believe as we do, it can impact our ability to articulate our faith. We are instructed to 'always be prepared to give an answer to everyone who asks you to give the reason for the hope that you have' (1 Peter chapter 3 verse 15), but where are we going to learn how do that when the question never comes up?

When we can take for granted the people around us already have the same basic knowledge we do, and speak the same language or use the same terminology, we don't need to be able to explain what we believe and why in ways that anybody can understand. We can assume that they will get the same references we do.

If we are used to people nodding in agreement when we talk about our faith, how are we going to handle genuine curiosity—or robust challenge? Most importantly, how will we be a light to the world when we are hiding that light under the shade of the company of fellow believers, or be salt that flavours the world when we stay in the shaker?

Expanding Our Horizons

I'd encourage everyone to take a look at their social circles, and see whether they are diverse and vibrant. If not, maybe it is time to expand your horizons and step outside that comfort zone. I know for myself it is a challenge, I have never been good at breaking into new social circles. Sometimes you will feel like you are stuck in the middle.

But when we do take that chance, it opens up a whole new world and lets us see things from a whole new perspective. And, most importantly, it shows us that people who believe differently—whether religion or politics or even taste in music—are just as human as we are.

Everywhere we look the world is increasingly being divided into camps, often hostile to one another. Let's do our part to break down barriers and create a world where there is no 'us versus them'—only 'us'.

WHO IS THE ANTICHRIST?

by Jeremy Dover

Fierce speculation surrounds the identity of the antichrist. The Book of Revelations points to an antichrist/s that opposes God's plan and stands in conflict against Jesus' people. Much of the morbid fascination comes from a misunderstanding of this book. In our culture we have little experience with apocalyptic literature and many ignore the importance of genre in helping to interpret meaning. For me, the whole book, with all its strange apocalyptic imagery, can be summarized in just two words: "Jesus wins!"

It is, however, curious to watch each generation 'guess' the identity of the antichrist. People try to interpret the Book of Revelations through the eyes of the newspaper rather than through the context of the whole Bible storyline. Moreover, the antichrist that appears repeatedly in the Bible is seen as anything, whether a person or a concept, that stands against Jesus. So, here is my guess as to one antichrist today. The one that shines bright in our Western society is the god of 'consumerism'.

Consumerism

Every 'ism' has positives and negatives. Capitalism promotes financial growth which raises living standards. However, it also gives birth to an egocentric hedonism called consumerism. The desire for more 'stuff' is a seductive mistress. Two examples highlight this: Halloween and Black

Friday.

Halloween

Halloween was once isolated to America and horror movies. However, it has established itself firmly in the Australian calendar. Why? Because we have a deep spiritual desire. No, not for the Roman Catholic All Saints Day or the ancestor worship of the 'Day of the dead'. Most people would have no idea or care about these backgrounds of Halloween.

It is more a deep spiritual need for a god that brings meaning. In this case, consumerism fills a desire to buy (plastic junk) and build a community around that. As Halloween approaches, scrutinize the huge weight of products on show and the social pressure to buy. This is a spiritual act beyond the argument about ghosts and goblins.

Black Friday

Black Friday in Australia was once a day to remember the 1939 Victorian bushfires that claimed 71 lives. However, through a George Orwellian 'new-speak' we now have a new meaning for Black Friday: to buy stuff. The day gives you permission to buy more! It might be a new toaster oven or a dress you do not need but consumerism becomes an idol. It is estimated that Australia's Black Friday sales of $400 million will surpass Boxing Day sales. As Black Friday approaches note the frenzy to consume.

Amnesia syndrome

This amnesia syndrome is a result of consumerism and makes us forget our Creator. It is an old god, or as the Book of Revelations puts it, another antichrist that dulls our senses to our deepest longing: a restored and fulfilling relationship with our Creator. This is, by definition, an antichrist.

Consumerism is subtle and appears harmless, not the scary beast we might expect. However, it dulls our memory of God and can, if not checked, distract us from the real meaning of life in its fullness. Like all sales strategies, it convinces us we can find meaning if we just have that product or service. The challenge is to take the positives of our financial blessings but not slide into the negatives that let it become an antichrist. It is about remembering that real meaning comes from following Christ not consumables.

SUPERMORALITY

by David Goodwin

Every writer dreams that they will create a character that will capture their reader's imagination, and endure. But when, in 1932, two young comic book writers came up with an idea for a new super hero, they could not have imagined that it would not only outlive them, but become part of culture itself.

I discovered Superman as a child and was immediately hooked. I devoured everything I could find and, years later when I had come to faith, I began to see that there are many elements in the Superman mythos that are of value to my Christian journey.

If you have timeless values, they will sometimes be out of step with the values of the world

One of the criticisms levelled at Superman is that he is a bit old fashioned. As comics moved with the times they, like the world, began to see moral choices not in black and white, but in shades of grey. It was at this time that we saw the emergence of anti heroes, super heroes who were just as likely to kill or maim villains and criminals as they were to arrest them. A character like Superman, who upheld values like truth and justice and adhered to a strict code of behaviour, seemed quaint in comparison, and decidedly uncool.

I am sure all of us can see parallels with Christianity. It used to be that in the Western world society took its values from the Church, but as the world has moved on this is no longer the case, and for a lot of people the things that we uphold as important no longer matter, and are seen as relics of the past. Some churches try and keep pace with this changing world, casting aside truths that don't match with the majority view, but I believe that this is a mistake.

If we believe that the truths that we adhere to are timeless then we have to accept that, as the world around us changes, we will be out of step with popular culture, that we will be mocked as old fashioned. But, just as Superman has managed to weather almost eighty years in the volatile comics industry, if we remain faithful to the core, timeless truths we hold dear we will endure and the Church will continue to outlive and outlast the things that are built on less solid foundations.

There is a right and wrong in the Universe and it is not that hard to tell the difference

One of my favourite Superman writers is Elliot S! Maggin, and there is a recurring quote running through his stories, that "there is a right and wrong in the Universe and it really isn't that hard to tell the difference between the two".

As much as we argue about different cultures and relative versus objective truth, it is plain to me from the conversations I have with people around me that we all have a basic understanding of right and wrong. So many times I hear the same comment, that "I don't really hold with that Church stuff, but I am a good person, I believe in God, I've never killed anyone, or steal stuff, or...".

In the comics Superman is faced with moral choices of vast significance but, even in the most complex of situations, it is plain to him what the right answer is. When confronted with something that doesn't have a simple answer we are easily tempted to compromise or talk about ends justifying means, as a way of abdicating our responsibility to make a choice. Superman looks past the peripheral issues and sees the heart of the matter, refusing to make excuses not to act.

Even though the fate of planets does not rest on my shoulders, I can still identify with him because every day I am presented with a thousand choices. While occasionally I might be faced with a complex scenario, usually it is not difficult for me to see which choice is right—the question is what I actually do.

Doing the right thing is not easy

A recent DC animated short, 'Superman/Shazam!: The Return of Black Adam', features Billy Batson, a young orphan living in poverty, who always tries to do right by others even when it puts him in danger.

Billy is granted magical powers and is able to transform into the superhero Captain Marvel (now called Shazam due to copyright issues!), and together with Superman battles the evil Black Adam. After much destruction and seeing Superman apparently killed, Captain Marvel has Black Adam at his mercy and is tempted to finish him once and for all. But in a wonderful speech, Superman tells him that "doing the right thing is not easy", and if it was, everyone would simply do it.

This really spoke to me, because it mirrors so completely what I see, not only in the world around me, but in my own life. Working out the right thing to do isn't usually all that hard, but actually doing it can be another thing entirely. It seems to me that the easiest option, the path of least resistance, is usually the wrong thing to do, which hardly seems fair. But, the lesson I take from Superman is that we do the right thing because it is the right thing to do, and therefore worth doing—not because it is easy.

We need heroes

It is easy for us to sneer at comics, and treat them as if they are something childish with little to teach us about life. But, as you hopefully have a sense of, they are full of truths that can speak to us all, whatever our age. We need heroes who inspire us to believe in something bigger than ourselves, and make us want to be better. And the greatest heroes share their virtues with Christ.

HOW OUGHT CHRISTIANS VOTE?

by Roydon Ng

Isn't it ironic that often the people who know least about Christianity insist that Christians must vote in a certain way?

Both the left wing and right wing of politics are often guilty of reducing Christians down to a group that impacts upon the final ballot count. The intersectionality of faith and politics has often been over-simplified even by Christians who label fellow believers ungodly merely because of their left- or right-wing electoral preferences.

It is uncomfortable to be challenging traditional stereotypes such as that Christians are all conservatives, but Christians can choose to have various political leanings for reasons that are deeply rooted in their faith.

A Christian's identity is in Christ

Christians should be careful not to use political motivations as justifications for their deeds of faith. Doing good in living for Jesus shouldn't be a part of a left-wing social justice ideology or in rebellion against the conservative right. A Christian's identity should be first and firmly in Christ above their different political leanings.

As part of daily devotions, Christians should assess themselves firstly in their relationship with God before deciding whether their candidates' positions are in line with Christian ethics and values.

Noting that the Bible doesn't speak directly to every modern political issue but rather provides timeless principles that cover a range of topics, living as citizens of God's kingdom Christians ought to be enhancing human life, human dignity and human rights.

Children and families make up essential cornerstones of our society which need to be strengthened along with gender equality and racial reconciliation. At the forefront of voting should be a preference for godly peace and justice not the political agendas of individuals, nationalist or interests that run against the common good.

Vote 1 for Jesus in your life, not a single issue at an election

As the political divide becomes more apparent and threats to religious freedom encroach on Christians once again, it is often easy to retreat into the corner of thinking that voting in one way or another will provide salvation for the church.

But Christians are called not to have a comfortable life rather one of suffering. Jesus has said that "If they persecuted me, they will persecute you" (John chapter 15, verse 20) and Paul reiterates this as he tells us that "Indeed, all who desire to live godly lives in Christ Jesus will be persecuted" (2 Timothy chapter 3, verse 12).

Thinking that we can vote our way out of suffering is trying to play Jesus for the church. How can Christians be a single-issue voter when there are always multiple issues that the Bible addresses that may be partially supported or opposed by a range of political candidates?

But more importantly, can Christians discount all other concerns for the sake of one issue, when the Bible speaks to many matters? No political party can be God—perfect in every Christian value or ideal.

Be immersed in prayer

How then can Christians act politically? Throughout our daily lives and not just leading up to elections, we pray that starting with ourselves we continually place our identity first and foremost in Jesus Christ.

Then we pray for our leaders, political parties and candidates that they may come to godly faith and finally, that Christianity is not exploited for partisan political agendas. God loves both voters of Liberal Party, Labor Party, and every other party and wants each of them to be in a relationship with Him. Our politics would be a much better place if Christians were less partisan and much more prayerful.

We can find comfort in the final words of Jesus as recorded in Matthew's gospel. Jesus is meeting with His disciples on the mountain and gives them instructions to go and make disciples for God's kingdom.

The Great Commission (Matthew chapter 28, verses 16-20) reminds us that the ultimate authority is Jesus and Christians are to share this message, not just back in their hometowns, but all over the world. It's not an easy command and not one that is done by relying solely on voting for a more Christian party or candidate.

It will require Christians to leave much behind, including our earthly political sympathies, as well as to face much struggle and opposition. But Jesus also gives us a great promise; that he will be with us always, to the very end of the age.

For everyone who calls themselves a follower of Jesus, it's not about whether you Vote 1 for a left- or right-wing party, Jesus cares about whether you've made Him number 1 in your life.

So as Christians go forth and make important decisions that affect the future of our country and the world, know that Jesus is with you. And that the Holy Spirit dwells in every believer and is active in guiding you as you lead others to Christ.

As Christians seeking to make the most out of difficult political situations, we have the assurance that we don't go in our strength, but prayerfully we have the support of the Jesus Christ because He is the One who has authority over heaven and earth.

THE ARMOUR OF GOD: BELT OF TRUTH

by Nic Lee

Stand firm then, with the belt of truth buckled around your waist, with the breastplate of righteousness in place, and with your feet fitted with the readiness that comes from the gospel of peace. (Ephesians chapter 6, verses 14–15 NIV)

The concept of the belt of truth is actually a much bigger deal than we realise. Part of the challenge is that in our modern society we have changed the understanding of a belt and the role it plays as a fashion accessory. In its true context, the belt is super important piece in the Roman armour. More closely thought of like today's garter belts or suspenders, the belt holds all the armour together.

In this way, the belt of truth, and God's truth holds everything together. The truth of the Gospel and God's teachings as recorded in the Bible all combine to create a holistic protection and defence in spiritual warfare. Do not underestimate the importance of God's truth in our lives.

One common phrase these days that gets thrown around, especially from non-believers, is that their truth is not our truth. Basically, the premise is that truth is subjective and not necessarily objective and absolute. The Christian position is actually quite unique when it comes to truth—we claim in Christ an absolute truth; He is the absolute truth.

Now, in order for anyone else to prove the reverse is to basically claim that there is no absolute truth, but the flaw in this argument is that this claim itself is an absolute truth. Let us leave the topic there because to venture further is a distraction from the main purpose of this article.

Application and Testimony

We have seen the importance of truth in recent times. It is often said that truth is one of the first casualties in politics. Contrast that to the teaching of Jesus where He proclaims Himself to be the Way, the Truth and the Life; that no one could come to the Father except through Him (John chapter 14, verse 6).

I was reading and studying from the book of Judges and one of the first lessons that we learn about Israel is that spiritual amnesia can lead to our destruction and suffering. The young nation had, within a generation, forgotten the truth of God's grace and actions in delivering them from Egypt, and as a result, God allowed them to be plundered.

When we fall into that trap and forget the truth of God's sovereignty and His divine work sometimes God will allow us to suffer. It is only with the belt of truth actively worn and applied over our lives that God will unveil our eyes to our sin and pride and enable us to repent and draw close to Him again.

Prayer

Dear God,

Thank you for all the times Your grace and love have been showered upon us. As we reflect on our lives, help us to recognise where Your truth and presence have been instrumental in our lives. Help unveil our eyes and hearts to the truth of who You are, and how You are working in and through our lives, as well as those around us. Thank you for sending us signs and wonders that give You the glory.

Lord, just as You value truth, help us to also align our heart and will to your own, where we can value the simple and convicting truths that are infused throughout Your Word. Jesus, as you once taught, You are indeed the Way, Truth and Light unto this world. As we meditate on this truth, reveal Yourself to us.

For some of us, we are confused and filled with doubt and uncertainty. It may relate to something we have heard, or even a perception or view we hold about a topic or person. Help us in this need where Your truth can shine through the mist and murkiness that is the confusion, doubt and uncertainty.

May Your truth not just protect and defend, but also be an active weapon that disarms lies, deceit and mistrust. Help us to equip ourselves and cover ourselves with Your righteous truth so that we can always respond in love and grace. The importance of Your covering which is founded in truth cannot be underestimated; Lord help us to fully appreciate the depth and seriousness of Your spiritual protection.

Holy Spirit, You delight in the warmth and light that is the truth. May You always be a constant presence in our lives so we know that we are walking in truth and not veering off the narrow path towards righteousness.

Lord help us to keep an open mind so that the truth will set us free from any bondages of the past. Sometimes our history is full of memories and ideas that we have formed based on our perception and limited perspective. Our emotions can sometimes cloud our judgement and distort our ability to accept the truth.

May Your truth prevail and be a light unto the world.
In Jesus Name, Amen.

> Don't let your heart be troubled
> Hold your head up high
> Don't fear no evil
> Fix your eyes on this one truth
> God is madly in love with you
> Take courage
> Hold on
> Be strong
> Remember where our help comes from
>
> (Good Grace, Hillsong United 2018, Joel Houston)

Section five

Visions and Dreams

GOD, THE STORY WRITER

by Kevin Park

Guess what the most famous Bible story is which doesn't include Jesus? Well, it's David and Goliath (1 Samuel chapters 16-17)!

David, the Giant Slayer

The story begins when Samuel listens to God about choosing David, a young shepherd, as the replacement for King Saul and as the next king of Israel. After anointing David as the next king privately, an evil spirit tormented Saul.

One of Saul's servants advises him that a musician, who can play the lyre, will help to soothe his spirit. Apparently, David was chosen to do it and, since Saul loved him so much, he became one of his armour-bearers and was called into service for Saul whenever he needed help.

Saul and the Israelite army were going to have war with the Philistines in the Valley of Elah. They chose one man to determine the result of their battle. The Philistines chose Goliath who had been a warrior since his youth.

Although Saul did not believe David could win any battle, David confidently stepped up with five smooth stones, a sling and a staff. David was certain that the living God will fight for him as God had previously given him the strength to rescue his sheep from bears and lions.

As soon as Goliath approached the battle to kill David, David calmly took one of the stones out of the bag and slung it at Goliath's forehead. The Philistine fell facedown on the ground and as a result, the Israelites won the battle.

The key message in this story is that we can be given the strength and power to overcome anything if we stand up with God by our side. 1 John chapter 5, verses 4-5 states that it is through faith. So, our faith can be seen as the stone in David's sling.

Obedience

Just like the Bible is full of stories, God writes our stories too. In fact, He knows them backwards as He planned how we are going to live from beginning to end (Psalm chapter 139, verses 13-16). It is just a matter of obedience whether we are going to follow Jesus Christ wholeheartedly or not.

The truth of Christianity is that we cannot be perfect through human effort. God does not judge us by perfectionism. This does not mean we are to be lazy and rely on God for everything.

Christ already made believers perfect in God's sight through His crucifixion and resurrection, and yet we are being made holy.

The meaning behind holiness is the idea of being different from how the world operates. Holiness naturally comes to believers but it also is a process in which the believer has to work through with the guidance of God's Spirit.

Put simply, we are not called to be perfect physically but we are able to be perfect spiritually by finding our identity in Jesus Christ and devoting our life to Him.

My Story

I am not physically perfect as I have disabilities in speech and on the left side of my body. Therefore, I use a speaking application or type what I want to say on my iPad and I have been learning how to be independent as much as possible.

After I became a Christian in 2011, I was baptised in 2012 and discovered a spiritual gift in 2013, which is Christian writing.

I have been writing devotionals to encourage others spiritually for over five years and now I have 11 platforms to do them on. In July of 2018, I joined Christian Today of New Zealand as a young writer. Due to my spiritual gift, I don't mind if I have some disabilities.

Although some people stare at me, I often offer grace to them by saying hello with a big smile. Nevertheless, I have a good community to be with and Jesus Christ as my Lord, Saviour and my best friend for the rest of my life.

Despite my time spent writing devotionals and articles, this doesn't mean I am a master in growing spiritually. The worldly life and Kingdom life have conflicting perspectives, and like most people, I have to work hard to make sure my worldly life doesn't overrule.

The world tells us that our minds could be healed by watching television. It also tells us that we can do whatever we want and that 24 hours is not enough time for a day.

However, the kingdom life prompts us that we could be truly healed through Jesus Christ and that we have to manage our time well as time belongs to God.

Conclusion

We do not have to get all acts together before following Jesus. He accepts where we just are. So, when we make a mistake, we have to acknowledge it, especially towards the Lord, and try again.

Just like David, I have been learning to bring God into every aspect of my life and, through Him, I can achieve anything.

For example, my little sister and mother have been better at English than me. As I keep practising my writing skills through devotionals, my mum has now been surprised at my writing skills, even if she cannot understand theology.

Instead of making our story through our efforts, let God be the story writer. Also, let us remember that He has a perfect plan for each of us (Jeremiah chapter 29, verse 11)!

A BEAUTIFUL REMINDER

by Elise Pappas

In April of 2018 a lovely friend gifted me the sweetest pair of little girl booties. We were not pregnant yet, but she gave them to me in faith, following the prompting of the Holy Spirit. I would keep these gifts in what would be her room. A room I would often be in, thanking Jesus for the little girl who we were believing for.

A few days ago, I was dressing our daughter Sophie, and I got to put these little booties on her. Tears streamed down my face as I distinctly remembered the night my friend gave them, the courage and faith that she had. I also remembered the countless times that we had prayed and believed for this little girl over the years and the heartache that we had experienced.

A few people have now asked me what it's like having Sophie—having received the miracle? I usually respond with—it is still surreal, and I actually don't ever want to allow it to become too familiar. Because I never want to forget all that Jesus has done for us. Holding her is like tangibly holding the goodness of God.

Did I believe that God was good before her? Absolutely. But she is just like this beautiful reminder of the goodness of God and His power that is at work in our lives.

We all need reminders

It is a good thing to be reminded of the goodness of God and His power that is at work in our lives. Because if He can do it in this area of our life, then He can certainly do it in other areas of our lives as well.

Reminders are one of those funny things, because in one day you can have any number of them. You can have reminders in your phone, alerts in your calendar, tasks on your to do list to jog your memory. Recently I was having coffee with a friend and as we were sitting there, their phone made a slurping noise. Laughingly, I asked my friend if it was their phone.

They explained that their doctor had encouraged them that they needed to drink three litres of water every day. This particular friend explained to me that the only way they were going to get through drinking that much water every day was to set a reminder on their phone. So that was what the slurping noise was about. They had downloaded an application where they could submit how much water they needed to drink per day, and it would give them regular reminders of when to drink.

We all have reminders of one thing or another, but what if we were that deliberate in being reminded about how good God has been to us? Imagine if we had set reminders to celebrate His goodness. My mother always would say to me that no matter what you are going through, there is always something to be grateful for.

A beautiful reminder is what our daughter has been to me. A beautiful reminder of His goodness and power that is at work in our life.

Set Reminders

We all have reminders; of people, places, times. Some are beautiful, others—not so much. But what I have learnt over this past few years is that when I decide to thank Jesus for all He has done in my life it helps me to forget about the petty things in life.

It's hard to be really thankful and negative at the same time. It's difficult to feel joy and deep sorrow at the same time. David writes in Psalm Chapter 34, verse 8 to 'taste and see that the Lord is good'. Jesus wants you and I to be able to testify of His goodness.

He wants us to be able to experience it first hand and encourage others with it. He not only wants us to be reminded of His goodness, but to remind others as well.

I was recently listening to one of Hillsong United's most recent songs called 'Ready or Not'. My favourite line of this song is 'bring Him praise for what He's going to do next'.

Whether we have received our miracle this side of heaven or not we can continue to thank Him for all He has done and be reminded of all that He is able to do next.

ARE YOU BRAVE AGAIN?
by Cartia Moore

The daring adventure of being brave seems to be such a simple concept in movies. That moment where an overwhelming sense of bravery overtakes a person, and they defeat the evil against them. It seems so simple and easy to follow. But it really isn't in real life.

Bravery is an incredible word that is used to describe a person's inner strength when it comes to certain challenges. When I think of the word bravery, it reminds me a lot of the quote by Eleanor Roosevelt that says, "You gain strength, courage and confidence by every experience in which you stop to look fear in the face".

Bravery is not about physical strength, it is not even about the level of one's capacity to run head-first into something dangerous. Bravery is the consistent mindset of a person when given a challenge to overcome, and they do it with an inner strength. This strength is given by God.

In C.S. Lewis's Prince Caspian, there is a quote that says,

> 'You have listened to fears, child,' said Aslan. 'Come, let me breathe on you. Forget them. Are you brave again?'

I love this quote because not only does it reflect what God is like to us, but it presents the idea that we are brave and strong because of God.

Believe

Reflecting on the year that has been, what I have done, what I could have done better, and how far I have come since this time last year, are huge things to reminisce about. One thing I keep having to remind myself of is to not be overwhelmed by the events of life. Life is built up of moments, good and bad, but they won't last forever.

The thing we, as children of God, need to always think about is how much He has planned for us. Our lives are full of abundance, but whether or not we choose to believe that, it will always affect our outlook on life.

Allow God

In moments where we can't seem to grab hold of our purpose, or our belief in the revealing of that job God promised us or that relationship we keep praying for, or that dream we hold onto ever so tightly, that is when we need to turn to God—to His Word, completely submissive, and give it all to Him.

The Bible says in Psalm chapter 37, verse 4, 'Take delight in the Lord, and he will give you the desires of your heart'. He knows our hearts and what lies beneath it. He knows what our dreams are and what we desire most. Why would the God of all creation ignore what sets our souls on fire?

When we doubt God's ability to provide, or to deliver what we have desperately been praying for for so long, we are actually depriving ourselves of great blessing and opportunity to witness God doing what he does best.

Putting aside all that corrupts the mind, the Bible says in 2 Corinthians chapter 10, verse 5:

> We demolish arguments and every pretension that sets itself up against the knowledge of God, and we take captive every thought to make it obedient to Christ. (NIV)

I must be obedient to God, and by following God's Word and listening to Him in every situation, I actually allow God in to make me brave.

I must also allow God to be God, without taking the power of the situation away from Him. By this, I mean, when we take what God has promised into our own hands, due to impatience or frustration, it never works out for us. The only way we see things come into prosperity and blessing is by giving all we pray for and desire in life to God, and allowing Him to take it in His hands and do with it what He wants.

Back seat driver

I have driven in my car many times with many different people, and one thing that always makes the journey a little more interesting is when I am driving with a back-seat driver. It is ironic because although they may know how to drive, I am the one in the front seat. Their life is in my hands, and whether or not we make it to our destination safely, comes from my ability to be able to drive, not the passengers.

Sometimes we treat God like this and we become the back-seat driver. God is a mystery, but He knows what He is doing. It doesn't matter how overloaded with emotion, anxiousness, stress, or frustration I am, the undeniable ability to believe in the promise that God will pull me through, is what I need to turn my focus to.

Romans chapter 8, verses 37 says:

> No, in all these things we are more than conquerors through him who loved us. (NIV)

What does it mean to be a conqueror? It means to defeat something that holds us back from something greater—to overcome. And God says that we are more than conquerors. But how are we more than conquerors? Through Him who loved us. We are nothing without God. But with Him, we have the potential to do anything!

Bravery may just be a word, but the meaning behind it means so much more to God than we realise. God is the bravery within us. He makes us strong and confident. He helps us when we are faced with adversity. He always wins, and as long as we are walking with Him, we will too.

Sit back, take a breath, and look at your obstacle. Do not fret, it is just a momentary struggle. Now tell it that your God has it handled, because He does, and my goodness, does He have an incredible plan for you. Focus on him.

> Be still and know that I am God.
> (Psalm chapter 46, verse 10 NIV)

Are you brave again?

A DRAWER CALLED OBLIVION
by Travis Barnes

At home I have a drawer called oblivion. Oblivion is the name of the drawer because in it are all kinds of things that are never to be seen again. The drawer is full of old mobile phone chargers, computer cables, various kinds of batteries and instruction manuals to appliances that I no longer own. My daughter ferrets around in oblivion and pulls out an old iPod.

"Daddy, Daddy I have my very own iPod!"

"That's nice," I tell her, "but it's just for pretending". For the battery ran flat some years ago.

But my daughter is undeterred: "Charge it Daddy! Charge the iPod!"

Now the iPod is eleven years old and surely hasn't been switched on for at least eight but having dug up its charger from the depths of oblivion the iPod awakens from its slumber. It was like opening a time capsule with songs from high school land songs that were once all the rage. It got me thinking: I wonder if there's a dream in the drawer?

A dream. Shoved in there years ago, not quite discarded, not quite dispensed with but almost entirely forgotten. What have you done with all the dreams that have died in your life?

My Dream

I was twenty-four years old when God gave me a dream to start a new Church in one of Victoria's poorest communities. Over the following months, the dream grew into an irrepressible vision to see a Church that wouldn't just have good news but be good news for the whole community. I read endless books about Church planting and talked to everyone I knew about my dream. I was youthful and eager, my heart full of hope and my head full of dreams; I was alive! It's a pity my dream did not survive.

Despite my best efforts and many prayers, the Church plant didn't work out the way I hoped. Truth be told, it didn't even come close. It was an unmitigated disaster; it felt like a complete and total failure. I packed up, moved away and put my dream in the back of the drawer never to be seen again.

Joseph's dream in the drawer

In the Old Testament Joseph has a dream that God is going to make him a great leader. No sooner has he had this dream he is sold into slavery by his brothers. Joseph serves as a slave in the house of Potiphar and is so successful he is put in charge of Potiphar's entire household. Joseph is a righteous man, and when he refuses to sleep with Potiphar's wife she makes false accusations and Joseph is thrown into prison. So much for the dream. You can read the full story in the book of Genesis, starting at chapter 37.

Holding onto God

There are some things we can learn from Joseph's experience. Firstly, even in tough times he continued to put his faith in God. Secondly, when in prison Joseph interprets the dreams of his fellow inmates. How would it feel helping other people with their dreams when your dreams have gone nowhere? Joseph didn't understand why his dreams had come to nothing but continued to serve the Lord regardless.

I had many questions for God when my dream fell on its face. Eventually I recognised that you can question God, or you can worship God, and so, despite my confusion, I decided to worship God. With our limited understanding we cannot always grasp God's eternal perspective.

Keep growing

Joseph continued to lead. He was put in charge of Potiphar's household and then later he was put in charge of all in the prison. Wherever Joseph was, he put his leadership into action. Joseph didn't wait around for leadership opportunities to fall out of the sky; he started where he was.

I've continued to develop my skills and knowledge as a Christian minister. Perhaps God will one day call upon the skills I've developed in connection with the dreams I had long ago. If not, I'll continue to serve God as diligently as I can wherever I find myself.

Waiting...

Finally, we can learn that Joseph waited. He didn't have any choice being in prison but wait he did. Do you think Joseph was a better leader because of the thirteen years of waiting that took place between Joseph's dream and its commencement? Abraham waited 25 years to become the Father of many nations as God had promised—was Abraham better for the wait? And, Moses spent 40 years waiting in the wilderness before God called him to lead the Israelites out of Egypt. C.S Lewis once said, "I am sure God keeps no one waiting unless he sees that it is good for him to wait".

Don't discard that dream in the drawer. You might need it soon.

INSPIRED BY A STEP OF FAITH

by Joseph F. Kolapudi

I've often found myself wondering why certain things are made to last, while others seem to fade with time. Stories of people through time who have been remembered, some who have been forgotten, and others whose stories are still to be told. The one thing that stands out amongst the tapestry of time is the inspiration that we all draw on to live out our wildest dreams.

When you think about it, there is a big difference between motivation and inspiration. Some people often are so motivated to do something—whether it is tackling a new hobby, or business venture, or adventure—but after considering the vast amount of information that we seem to consume day in and day out give up almost instantaneously. It is easy to become demotivated—but who ever thought of becoming de-inspired? There's no such word. The truth is, inspiration can last a lifetime.

Recently, I was talking with a friend, who also happens to be an avid blogger, about the infamous issue of 'writer's block'. Now, for all of you out there who have yet to experience this frustrating onset of feverish ineptitude and incapacity for creativity, count yourselves lucky. But my blogger friend revealed something that got me thinking. When speaking of her creative process, she said, "you just need to look around you—the world is full of inspiration". It was just the reminder I needed.

The truth is, there can be more than one source of inspiration. It is not something that one can find simply by reading a one-line quote, or by attending an informational seminar—it is something that one encounters during a moment in time. Perhaps it is hearing someone's story, or experiencing something spectacular, or even listening to a conversation and being lost for words—what occurs during that moment in time is sure to outlast any experience you have ever encountered before.

I still recall the moment when I first heard the story of an American missionary pilot who flew into the jungles of South America, only to be captured by guerrillas and taken hostage against his will. After several days, on the brink of desperation and despair, he finally had the courage to escape, and lived to tell the story. Although I was only in primary school when I first heard this story, it was the catalyst that sparked my journey of missionary service, and is one story that has stuck with me since—even though as I write this, I am on the other side of the world and in a completely different reality.

The amazing thing is, the source of inspiration that draws one life to another is the same Source that continues to inspire countless generations into living lives that are worth something greater than life itself. It is this inspiration that makes people give up their career, or their car, or their very carefully planned lifestyle, to embrace a lifelong calling that is beyond what they could have ever asked for or imagined.

What is your inspiration? Maybe it means giving up the pursuit of something you think you want for something you know you need. Perhaps it requires sacrificing your future plans in order to realise your dreams. It could even cost you something that you know you could never go back to. The only way to really know is to take that step of faith—the outcome is sure to surprise you.

STEP INTO THE LIGHT
by Kristen Dang

What are we like under pressure, when there is nowhere to hide? Are we the same whether or not the spotlight of humanity's torch is focused on us? Do our lives reflect the eternal light of Christ alive in us? We are all witnesses, whether we like it or not, and we are all seen and fully known by God.

Everything seen, nothing hidden

Serving on the worship team at my local church, I find myself acutely aware of both my weaknesses and my strengths. There is a team around me and, as we worship our God, we also support one another to minister to the congregation.

I am surrounded by people who love God and are glad to give Him glory in all they do. Their testimonies, marked by a choice to surrender what they have to God and let Him move, have encouraged me. I have seen my brothers and sisters choose to worship in sickness, fatigue, uncertainty, and even in seemingly missed opportunities, just as much as they have when they have been going from strength to strength.

In Psalms, it says:

> My frame was not hidden from You,
> When I was made in secret,
> And skilfully wrought in the lowest parts of the earth.

> Your eyes saw my substance, being yet unformed.
> And in Your book they all were written,
> The days fashioned for me,
> When as yet there were none of them.
> (Psalm chapter 139, verses 15-16 NIV)

God created us all in His beauty, fully equipped with everything we need for the days He has fashioned for us. That means He already knows our weaknesses before we discover them, and He knows where we will find our gifts. I have been nervous, uncertain if I was the right person for the task, and laughed at the thought that God might want to use me in a certain way, but in the end I know He will never ask me to do something He won't help me to do.

I can make that choice to trust God, and that is the choice I want to make every time I step on stage for a service—to surrender to God and let Him use me. He knows me completely and whether in weakness or in strength, I know that everything within me was made to give Him praise!

The spotlight we choose

One thing I love about our church worship team is the humility I see. Here are people willing to serve with everything God has given them, yet also willing to lift others up in order to help them exercise their Spirit-given gifts. It shows hearts that are focused not on self-glorification, but on loving God, and loving others—hearts obedient to the desires of God, and not those of the world.

> ...For the Lord does not see as man sees, for man looks at the outward appearance, but the Lord looks at the heart.
> (1 Samuel chapter 16, verse 7 NIV)

We can choose to live right by the world's standards, or live right by God, and the consequences of that choice will not be hidden. The world's spotlight is greedy and easily distracted. It is something that costs time, energy, and personal integrity as we chase after its insatiable promises to make us anything and everything.

In contrast, God's spotlight simply promises to show us who He has made us to be—children of God, loved by Him. It is not a spotlight we need to chase, but one that is always shining. All we need to do is drop the barrier, drop the pretence, drop the mask, and let God show us who we were made to be.

Dare to reveal

It can be a scary thing to step into the light. Our weaknesses are made visible, and our hearts are laid bare. Yet, there is blessing in all this. As our weaknesses are revealed and handed over to Christ, they are transformed by His strength. As our hearts are laid bare before Him, they are filled to overflowing with the measure of His love. Failures are transformed into testimonies, mourning into joy, tiredness into wings like eagles that rise up and are even able to carry others into the embrace of Christ.

When Christ has given us life, why should we be afraid to celebrate? When Christ has given us freedom, why should we be afraid to rejoice? When Christ has lifted us out of the waters and onto the rock of His strength, why should we hold back from declaring His victory?

Don't be afraid to let God shine! We are all called to be His witnesses, so let us bless His name with all that we are!

> Bless the Lord, O my soul;

And all that is within me, bless His holy name!
(Psalm chapter 103, verse 1 NKJV)

SERVING FROM A WHEELCHAIR

by Manuele Teofilo

For most of my teenage years, I felt like I wasn't serving in my local church. Even thought that I couldn't serve in any of the ministry teams. I didn't know what skills I had that could be used in a ministry team.

Let's see... Having limited music skills meant that I couldn't join the worship team. Be a youth leader, if I couldn't run around and play highly active games for fun then I won't be able to do so with the younger youth.

There was the welcome team on Sunday mornings greeting people as they enter church, but I didn't think people would understand my speech.

A teenage Christian in a wheelchair

I was a teenager, which meant that my self-confidence was low. Being a Christian made me want to serve in a church ministry. Like my peers, they were in the music team, youth leaders or serving some other way in church. However, almost all the ministries they served in involved practical tasks.

I was a teenage Christian in a wheelchair, so I was usually on the receiving end of practical love and care of others. It was difficult to think of times when I showed practical love to others. Or think of ways I could practically fill a need of another person.

As a teenager, my understanding of serving and showing love was limited to practical actions. That's how Samoan culture and how I thought NZ society defined love and care. So, helping set up and pack down at church events and serving food and drinks are things I saw as serving.

Forms of showing love

I placed a lot of weight on 'hands on' services. I was naïve in my thinking that just listening to people and speaking words of encouragement doesn't have much significance. Something effortless to do but it can have a great impact on people.

These are things I'm able to do and loved doing. However, I belittled these acts of love and didn't count them as ways to serve the church. I was too focused on trying to fit into one of the 'practical' ministries in my local church.

One day in my late teen years I had a catch up with a mentor. I shared with him the frustrations I had earlier that day. My mother was cooking a Samoan dish which is very laborious to prepare. I felt helpless and guilty sitting in my chair wanting to provide extra hands. But the most I could practically do is watch.

As mentors often do, pointing out your blind sides or offering a different perspective. My recollection is that he told me about how standing by and watching can be an important task. When I just watch I can spot minor details people may not be aware of or miss. Then I have the responsibility of, for example, pointing out that it's time for a batch of Mum's cooking to come off the stove.

I felt encouraged by my mentor's response. It was then when I started to put more weight on the small ways of showing love and serving the church community. By small ways, I mean non-practical forms of love.

Loving in ways I can

"You can't give what you don't have", is a phrase you hear when having discussions about donating money. But I didn't grasp the concept of the phrase as a teenager in a wheelchair. If I don't know how to play a musical instrument, then how will I ever be in the worship team?

The phrase implies that I should focus on the skills that I have and serve in ways that I can. In ways like offering to pray for people. Praying or spending time with people are some things I can do to show love and care for people in my community.

My way of showing love to family, friends and church community may not be the typical way, but it is my way. Life is different when you're in a wheelchair, so I have different needs. Just as much as I have different skill sets that I can use to bless others, if people allow me to.

What we have to offer

We all have skills, talents and abilities that we can use to serve our neighbours. But it isn't just our skills and resources that we offer to others. Rather, it is the gift of God's love in us that we offer through our acts of kindness.

No matter what we do to serve people in our lives, we all do it for the same reason. It is because we are excessively loved by God who created us and saved us.

So, instead of getting caught up in figuring out how I can serve my community. I can allow the love I receive from Christ to drive me to love people. Letting Him lead me in how I serve. At the end of the day, the best thing I can offer to anyone is His love.

IF YOU'RE NOT COMFORTED BY REVELATION YOU'RE READING IT WRONG
by Jessica McPherson

Until I came to university I used to think that Revelation was equal parts scary and confusing but at least it was at the end of the Bible so you could somewhat avoid it for the most part. I did feel a bit bad about that but I also did not know how to read the book especially with all the unhelpful information that was out there about Revelation—for example the idea that credit cards were the mark of the beast! Then God blessed me with a church that taught about Revelation in a clear and comforting way, parting the curtain of fear and confusion and letting in the beautiful light of the gospel.

The Genre of Revelation

One of the first things I learnt about how to properly read Revelation was that Revelation, like the rest of the Bible, told the story of the Gospel! A reading of Revelation without the gospel was not Revelation at all! The Gospel news of our sin, God's judgement & mercy, and our forgiveness and reunion into relationship with God is threaded throughout the entire Bible from the Garden of Eden to the garden city in the new heavens and new earth.

The thing that is different about Revelation is how it tells the

Gospel which is "like an impressionist painting", the genre of Revelation is apocalyptic literature which is vivid and full of pictures and powerful images. It is different from other parts of the Bible such as the writings of Moses—history and law, or Psalms—poetry. Revelation is not meant to be read from start to finish with the reader expecting a straightforward historical account of what will happen in the future.

The Purpose of Revelation

Revelation was first sent to the 1st Century Christians, these fellow believers from the past were already facing seemingly insurmountable challenges to their faith and daily lives so it seems a bit harsh if on top of that they were given a frightening and confusing book to study. However, if it was actually a message of great hope and comfort encouraging them to persevere and keep on amongst struggles, a message that was full of helpful instruction and wonderful pictures of the amazing reward God had in store for them, then it makes a lot more sense!

The purpose of Revelation was never to fill people with dread or confusion but the exact opposite! It was to bring comfort to the suffering and persecuted, and re-state God's wonderful promises for those who trust in him! It is written in a different way than most of the other books in the Bible but the core message of the Gospel is the same.

The Book of Revelation has scenes of judgement but they are not meant to terrorise believers, they are to show that those that do evil (such as the Roman emperors who were torturing and killing many Christians) would face God's judgement and would not escape punishment even if it looked like they would. God was showing the heavenly plan that transcended all time as opposed to just what we simply see from our earthly perspective.

Some of the scenes of judgement were to warn Christians to be on their guard against sin, encouraging them to stay firm in their faith even as they knew that they were being held on to tight by their Heavenly Father who would not let them go. In short, Revelation was retelling the story of sin and judgement, mercy and forgiveness, and God's sovereignty over all!

The Comfort of Revelation

One of the promises of God that I dwell on the most is that He will return and set everything right at the end of time! He will uphold the cause of the victim and bring justice; he will make everything as it should be and end all pain and suffering. There is a beautiful verse that encapsulates this in Revelation chapter 21 verse 4,

> He will wipe every tear from their eyes. There will be no more death or mourning or crying or pain, for the old order of things has passed away. (NIV)

What a beautiful picture! Never to cry or mourn or hurt again!

Yet it gets even better than that—in verse 3, the one just before that verse, it says,

> And I heard a loud voice from the throne saying, "Look! God's dwelling place is now among the people, and he will dwell with them. They will be his people, and God himself will be with them and be their God." (NIV)

There will be no grief and we will be in perfect relationship with God and his people!

There are so many beautiful pictures in Revelation about what it will be like when Jesus returns and the purpose of them is to amaze us at God's indescribable nature, His love for us, and the fact that even amidst the severest persecution we can trust that God is sovereign, He does know what is going on and he cares for us more deeply than we can ever know.

Section six

Intentionality

THE ME I USED TO BE

by Travis Barnes

I've kept a diary everyday for twenty years. This means that I have diaries strewn across my house. I'm not a very good minimalist. Reading my diaries from my teenage years is somewhat cringeworthy; my taste in music was certainly questionable. I'm struck however by how passionate I was to know and serve God. I didn't necessarily pray or read Scripture to a heroic extent.

Like many teenagers I had moments of great enthusiasm followed by periods of inconsistency. I was hungry though; hungry for more of God in my life. I was passionate about my Church and my youth group, and after my first taste of Scripture Union missions I was fired up to know Christ and make him known. In my early twenties I was someone who would go anywhere and give everything for the sake of God's kingdom.

Low ebbs

Whilst I've never experienced walking out on God, like many I've experienced low ebbs in my Christian journey. There have been times that I've looked back at and felt that I'm not the passionate Christian I once was, my diaries become a reminder of the me I used to be. What do we do when we wake up and realise that we lost the passion for Christ that we once had? How do we rekindle the passion that once set our hearts ablaze?

Allow me to share two thoughts to help us preserve and rekindle a passionate faith.

Is my faith in Christ alone?

Our faith must rest solely in Jesus. Not in our Church or a ministry we're excited about or a significant leader that we look up to. Our mentors will eventually disappoint us. Our Churches and its ministries will at some point dishearten us. In my early twenties I was very passionate about building Scripture Union mission teams and many of those teams were thriving at that time. Inevitably though, some key people moved on to other things, some of those teams began to struggle and some wound up entirely.

I've had important mentors who have let me down and some who abandoned the mission of Jesus altogether. I've watched Churches surging along doing great things only to see sin and division grind those thriving Churches to a halt. When our Churches, ministries, and mentors fail, will your faith rest solely in Jesus?

Jeremiah shows us how

Jeremiah is known as the weeping prophet; he spent his difficult life warning his people about the coming destruction of Jerusalem because his people had drifted from God. How did Jeremiah remain strong when his nation was falling apart? Jeremiah said these words:

> Blessed is the one who trusts in the Lord,
> whose confidence is in him.
> They will be like a tree planted by the water

that sends out its roots by the stream.
It does not fear when heat comes;
its leaves are always green.
It has no worries in a year of drought
and never fails to bear fruit.
(Jeremiah chapter 17, verses 7-8 NIV)

Becoming disillusioned

Jeremiah doesn't place his faith in his nation or the Kings who ruled it. Likewise, we should not place our faith in flawed mentors or fallible Church communities. God is the only one who will never fail us. He is the only one who we should put all our hope and trust in. When Churches fail, people sometimes lose their faith in God but that suggests their faith was misplaced.

People who experience the failures of the Church will often describe feeling disillusioned. Becoming disillusioned is better than it sounds because it means you're no longer living under an illusion. I was previously under an illusion that Christians would always do the right thing. I now realise that Churches are communities of flawed people who are on a transformational journey toward becoming like Christ. We should recognise that God is grieved by sin and wrongdoing, even when committed by Churches or Christians.

Forgiveness matters

When Christians have hurt me, I've held onto offence for far too long. It's been said that unforgiveness is like drinking poison hoping the other person dies. Holding onto offence was punishing me twice over; I was first mistreated and second by holding onto offence I was becoming bitter and angry.

Unforgiveness is an area when many Christians lose their passion because their hearts have become bitter. Forgiveness really is unlocking the door to the cell to discover that the prisoner was you! Paul urges in Colossians chapter 3, verse 13:

> Bear with each other and forgive one another if any of you has a grievance against someone. Forgive as the Lord forgave you. (NIV)

Rekindling a vibrant faith

How can we rejoice that Christ has forgiven us from the enormity of our sins while we stubbornly hold onto to the sins committed against us? Forgiving others will set us free and help us to rekindle a rich and vibrant walk with God.

YOUR CALLING DOES NOT SAVE YOU

by Blake Gardiner

When we consider either contemporaries or historical figures whom we admire, we tend to gravitate to their lived vocations. Consider Paul, one of our greatest missionaries, or Charles Spurgeon, dubbed the Prince of Preachers. When they come to mind, we often perceive their legacy through their calling or vocation.

While their works are admirable, if we are not careful, this frame of mind can lead us to not only idolise others and hamper our faith, but could also shipwreck us spiritually. Bear with me.

Comparisons

We live in a world of social media and comparisons. It is becomingly dangerously easy to think less of ourselves within the space of a scroll of a few seconds as we scroll through our newsfeeds. While we are continually reminded in church of the dangers of social media and our identities in Christ, we forget the very tendency to mimic this behaviour before the pulpit.

One need only remain in a local church until this begins to emerge. As people serve in different capacities, we begin to equate spirituality and godliness with the tally of ministries we serve or the number of clocked hours at church in a week. But it doesn't stop there. Our churches are filled, and beautifully so, with individuals determined to advocate for others. Large chunks of our congregations are easily comparable to a College of Health cohort. Yet not all, and so we compare our vocations outside of church. Some are deemed more noble than others. And so, we compare again, considering some more like Christ because of their profession.

This correlation between a Christian faith and a vocation of self-sacrifice is not foreign to the Gospel. In James 2, we are continually reminded of the importance of substantiating faith with action. Throughout the Gospels, Jesus continually reminds His audience to not only hear His words, but to also obey. Yet, as someone who has often been on the receiving end of these comparisons, I feel we are gravely missing the point when we think more highly of others because of their ministry involvement or profession.

The Temptation of Self-Righteousness

In the 2008 film, *Fireproof*, Caleb Holt (Kirk Cameron) considers himself a heroic firefighter, striving to put others' safety above himself. All the while, he is a deplorable husband through his unkindness, anger, and infidelity. Yet, Holt's profession blinds him to his moral wretchedness, and he remains convinced that because of his profession, his actions at home are excused.

If I'm being frank, the temptation to think this way plagues me every day. It is far too easy to assume that the societal notion that my profession is noble excuses my lack of humility before God. In Matthew chapter 19, Verse 24 we are familiar with Jesus' saying,

> Again I tell you, it is easier for a camel to go through the

eye of a needle than for a rich person to enter the kingdom of God. (ESV)

While the literal interpretation is clear and the New Testament is littered with warnings regarding material wealth, C.S. Lewis' commentary in *Mere Christianity*, paints a convicting warning for the church: You are quite likely to believe that all this niceness is your own doing, and you may easily not feel the need for any better kind of goodness. Often people who have all these natural kinds of goodness cannot be brought to recognize their need for Christ at all until one day, the natural goodness lets them down, and their self-satisfaction is shattered. In other words, it is hard for those who are rich in this sense to enter the kingdom.

As Lewis reminds us, if we think highly of ourselves because of our actions, we are prone to self-righteousness and a misplaced sense of independence from the grace of Christ. Ultimately, we begin to create a works-based salvation whereby we feel justified because of our actions and service, rather than by the atoning death of Christ.

The Work of the Spirit

This realisation is a two-fold blessing. As we draw away from letting our vocation define us as Christians, we begin to remember our daily need for confession and grace to grow in Christ by the Spirit. We are reminded that it is the Spirit who makes us like Christ, and our actions serve an outpouring of that process.

Secondly, we remember that we ought not to think of others as godlier because of their profession or ministry involvement, and we ought not to think less of ourselves because we are not thought of in the same way. We are all incredibly in need of grace, regardless of how godly, noble, or Christ-like we may appear. Everyday, the Spirit reminds us that the only way we may grow in godliness is through His power alone and, in this, we can rejoice.

WHY A LOVING GOD CAN'T JUST LET EVERYONE INTO HEAVEN

by Jessica McPherson

"If God is loving then why does he send people to Hell?" is a question that many people struggle with. It is a very important question because Heaven, Hell, and the character of God are all extremely important topics to consider and they have huge implications for how we live our lives.

I'm going to discuss the issue in two parts, firstly by talking about why people go to Hell and secondly by talking about why people go to Heaven.

Why some people go to hell and why I think it is unfair

I am convinced it is unfair that some people go to hell—but not for the reasons you might think. I think it is unfair that ONLY some people go to hell—we ALL deserve to go to hell and be separated from God's love.

Everyone has sinned by rejecting God, rebelling against him and committing evil in a multitude of ways that stem from our initial rejection of him. As Paul says in Romans chapter 3, verses 10–11, 'No one is righteous, no, not one; no one understands; no one seeks for God'.

And in Ephesians chapter 2, verse 1, 'As for you, you were dead in your transgressions and sins'. There is no one on earth who deserves to go to heaven for we have all sinned against God and whether we have done what we think are big sins or little sins we have all sinned and therefore are disqualified from getting into heaven.

Yet the amazing, incredible, MIND-BLOWING news of the Bible is that, even though we keep sinning and rejecting God, He continues loving us! He remains faithful to us and He even goes so far as coming to Earth as a human being and dying an excruciating and humiliating death on a cross so that we can be made right with him. He makes a way for us to have a restored relationship with him and access to heaven when we die!

Why some people go to heaven and why I think that is fair

God is all-powerful and he is in charge of everything so surely he could just let everyone into Heaven without Jesus dying and without people going to hell. Right? On the surface this seems like a good idea: no one suffers, no one dies, and everyone lives happily ever after… Except…

If this were the case, there would be no consequences for people who have done terrible evils. What about Pol Pot? He caused the death of 25% of the Cambodian people in his four year reign and died at his home aged 72 from suspected heart failure. Or Hitler? He was responsible for the deaths of over 19 million civilians and prisoners of war and committed suicide before his capture.

If there were no consequences, then there would be no justice for the victims of domestic violence, hit-and-runs, or sexual attacks. There would be no justice for people who have had their savings stolen, their houses burnt down, or their children abducted. When faced with such horrors we demand justice and rightly so, and sometimes people do get punished in this life, but what about when they don't? Is it right that Pol Pot didn't suffer any consequences? Is it right when a murderer or a rapist gets only a three-year prison sentence?

To say that those things do not matter and that there does not need to be any consequences for them is a horrifying idea. It does not make God more loving if he ignores sin—it actually makes him less loving—it means he does not care about justice and does not care about the victims. God MUST punish sin or else he is going against his character, which is loving; part of loving is requiring justice for wrongdoing.

It is not just the murderers and dictators who have sinned, but every person, as we have all rejected God, our Creator and LORD of all creation. Yet God loves us SO much that he sent his one and only son—Jesus—God the Son—to Earth to die for us! Jesus voluntarily gave up the glory of heaven to come to Earth as a human being (though still God) and die for us! In this way, God satisfies the need for justice and shows his AMAZING, INCREDIBLE, MIND-BLOWING love for us!

Now we need only accept Jesus' death for us, repent and follow him and we can be made right with God and have eternal life! As Paul says in Romans chapter 5, verse 8, 'But God shows his love for us in that while we were still sinners, Christ died for us.'

The perfection of the Cross

In the Cross of Christ we see mercy and justice come together perfectly to represent the enormity of God's love for us. A love so great that it cannot stand our sin against God or each other and demands justice, but also so great that He voluntarily stood in our place and took the punishment we deserve so we could inherit eternal life and be with Him forever!

As we go about our daily lives, let us take comfort in the fact that God brings justice to the victimised, joy in the fact that He sent His son to die for us, and hope in the fact that God can save whomever he chooses. May this spur us on to keep praying for and evangelising loved ones who don't yet know and trust in our Lord and Saviour Jesus Christ.

BECOMING DELIBERATE

by Rebecca Moore

Who knows how quickly a week can pass and you haven't stopped for a breath? "Oh look, it's Thursday already!" I often hear myself say, and it only feels like a couple of days since I said it a week earlier. If we're not careful, weeks turn into months and years, and we hardly notice.

Being deliberate

When my teenagers return to school following holidays, I miss them. I miss having them around, going on bushwalks and picnics together and planning family activities that we don't make the deliberate effort to do quite so often during the school term.

I find that during the first couple of weeks into the school term, I am deliberate in my interactions with my children outside of school/work hours: I will spend deliberate time chatting with them after school; I will spend deliberate time saying goodnight to them at bedtime; and I will spend deliberate time being interested in organising purposeful weekend activities.

Fast forward three or four weeks and I find myself back in the rat-race of regular activities, the motion of repetition, the familiar and thoughtless rut of routine and, before I know it, I have to snap myself out of it and remind myself to be deliberate again. Anyone relate?

Work it into your day

To help combat this run-ragged routine, my eldest daughter and I realised we needed to exercise to keep our minds and bodies fresh and alert. We knew the only way we could commit ourselves to exercising regularly was to work it into our day. It would need to be somewhere easily accessible; at the same time; and not overwhelming so as to put us off or seem too difficult. We would need to be deliberate.

By exercising together, we kept each other on task, and before we knew it, we had kept this daily event for four consecutive months! We have now developed a habit, and what felt like something we had just begun, we now realise those days turned into weeks which turned into months and will hopefully turn into years.

How deliberate are we when it comes to God?

Though I find myself chatting with God often throughout the day, being deliberate in prayer time can sometimes be an area vulnerable to distraction.

I was recently reading in Exodus about the Tent of Meeting. This is where Moses would meet to enquire of the Lord. This was a very deliberate place for Moses to meet with God, so much so, that whenever Moses entered the tent:

> ...the pillar of cloud would come down and stay at the entrance while the Lord spoke with Moses.
>
> Whenever the people saw the pillar of cloud standing at the entrance to the tent, they all stood and worshiped,

each at the entrance of their tent. The Lord would speak to Moses face to face, as one speaks to a friend'. (Exodus chapter 33, verses 9-11 NIV).

Moses would talk with God and God would answer him. They would have conversations 'face to face, as one speaks to a friend'. How awesome is that!

Sometimes we forget that, because of Jesus' sacrifice to banish the divide between God and His children, we have that same access where we can speak to God as a friend—the holiest of holy friends!

What does your Tent of Meeting look like?

Thinking on these things, I have begun writing a prayer journal again. For me, this has become my Tent of Meeting. This is where I write to God and He answers me, sometimes while I am still writing, other times a bit later. We have conversations which go beyond the paper, but the act of writing causes me to be deliberate in my thoughts and words. Because I like writing, this works well for me and I can return to previous prayers and see how they have been answered.

What does your Tent of Meeting look like, or what could it look like? You may prefer to incorporate your prayer in a deliberate daily prayer walk as a few of my close friends like to do. It may look different again to that, but whatever your chosen Tent of Meeting looks like, make it deliberate, make it regular and meet 'face to face, as one speaks to a friend' with the Creator God who longs to talk with you and be involved with your daily life.

At first it may need scheduling to help make it a routine,

but whether you put it in your diary or on an alarm on your phone, turn it into a habit and before you know it, those days will have become weeks, months and years and you will have amazing answered prayers to celebrate all the way through; prayers that will change the course of your future and the future of others.

> Therefore I tell you, whatever you ask for in prayer, believe that you have received it, and it will be yours. (Mark chapter 11, verse 24 NIV)

GO AND SEE THE STARS

by Matthew Thornton

A few weeks ago, I went on a weekend trip to a small NZ town called 'Mangakino' located on the North Island.

Living in Auckland, with all its light pollution, means I often don't pay attention to the evening sky. The reason—it just isn't that spectacular. Most of the stars aren't visible so it doesn't make for great viewing.

But, Mangakino,...well, that's a different story. The town is hours away from any major developments and is quite remote—meaning light pollution is minimal. This results in a spectacular night sky. I sat outside, braving the cold, for hours on end, overawed with its beauty and its magnificence.

It's not hard to find pictures of the evening sky on Instagram or online, and these pictures look incredible. However, nothing compares to seeing it in person. A wonder is evoked which simply cannot be replicated by its digital version.

What's more, the longer I sat there, and as my eyes began to the adjust to the light, the more stars I started to see. It was if the sky was unravelling before me. Crazy to think that same sky is above me right now, hidden beneath the veil of light pollution cast by city.

Funnily, it made me think: isn't this how it is with the God and His Spirit?

He is always present

Just like those stars, God's Spirit is always present, and He is continuously active in lives (1 John chapter 3, verse 24). Yet, often, He is drowned out by hustle and bustle, the busyness of life, the city lights. All it takes is for us to step back, get rid of those distractions and things which drown out God, and, suddenly, we will see the world like we've never seen before.

Taste and see

My night of star gazing also got me thinking about a point raised by a popular NZ musician: Strahan Coleman. He argues that, in our contemporary Christian culture, a 'knowledge-based' faith is promoted over a 'spiritual-based' faith.

Today, information is so rapidly disseminated and easily accessible that we have associated knowledge with the quantity of information an individual knows.

We have made the assumption that the amount we know about God, about the Bible, is directly proportional to our closeness with Him. Reading the Bible, Christian books and listening to podcasts are promoted over silent meditation and prayer.

Now, I'm certainly not trying to denounce intellectualism. I, myself, love uncovering the Bible's nuances and symbolism, and find it brings me closer to God. Having an intimate knowledge of the 'sword of the Spirit, which is the word of God' (Ephesians chapter 6, verse 17b) guides me in times of uncertainty. Rather than undermining intellectualism, what I am trying to say is this—there is more to knowing God than merely knowing about God.

Lessons from Job

Something that confounded me upon realisation was that Job is the first book of the Bible ever written. He was described as someone 'blameless and upright' (Job chapter 1, verse 1) before God. He knew God and was close to Him, as is evident in his faith through the trials and tribulations he faced. Astoundingly, he achieved all this without any literature about God, and without a Bible.

He had no choice but to find God spiritually. Yes, there would have been countless oral stories passed down through generations, and this would have helped. But all you need to do is play a game of 'broken telephone' to realise that oral stories are largely prone to distortion and corruption.

He wouldn't have been able to take each story he heard about God at face value, like we can in the Bible. He would have had to discern the truth of a story using what he already knew about God, through spiritual communion, as a reference.

Unlike Job, we have a Bible that is just a few clicks away. Unfortunately, we can often settle for complacency. It's easy to just settle for the Bible and not seek genuine communion with God. It's easy to make the knowledge about God the end, instead of God Himself.

Go and see the stars

Just like that Mangakino night sky, we could see countless pictures of the stars, and have numerous people describe these stars in detail to us. But until we truly see them and experience them for ourselves, there will always be so much beauty and wonder that we are missing out on.

How can we know the 'peace that passeth all understanding' (Philippians chapter 4, verse 7) if we restrict our faith to merely an intellectual experience of Him?

I, like Strahan, would like to challenge us to seek real communion with God. Let's really seek His Spirit. Ridding ourselves of the distractions, let's fix our gaze towards the heavens, and strive to get to know God, not simply about God.

When we allow God's Spirit to shine, to illuminate our lives, the world will unravel before us in a beauty and wonder that we cannot yet comprehend, nor yet know.

WORDS, AND HEARING THE VOICE OF GOD

by Cartia Moore

Words have so much power. One line from Star Wars can change the whole face of the storyline. "Luke, I am your father" – Darth Vader. What an absolute shocker that was.

I am always astounded by the power of the voice and of words. Proverbs chapter 15, verse four, says:

> Gentle words are a tree of life; a deceitful tongue crushes the spirit. (NLT)

There is power in words themselves, but there is also power in the way that they are said.

There is a song by Hawk Nelson that says, "Words can build you up, words can break you down, start a fire in your heart or put it out". The undeniable truth is that words are powerful.

The swift gentle response to an angry heart. The fired up and demanding roar of a justice-led politician. The determined and enthusiastic words from a passion-driven person. It is incredible the effect they can have on a person.

His Voice

I love reflecting on stories in the Bible of God's voice such as in Genesis chapter one. God's voice was the catalyst for change as He called the universe into being and whispered the breath of life into the world.

There is power in the voice of God. When God spoke, the universe was created. When He spoke, we were called into being as children of God. The voice that declared the stars be brought into being and scattered across the sky had a perfect plan for the universe.

The incredible thing is, that voice is not void, that voice is constantly in communication with us every day. We can hear this voice within everything that goes on in our lives.

The soft whisper

Often times when God moves in our lives, it is a soft whisper with a large effect. During the recent election, my family and I experienced the power of God's voice as He spoke into the hearts of pastors and church members who helped us throughout our campaign.

This was such a treasured and heart-warming experience, and as each of these people put their hand up to help, we felt the presence of God very closely. God was in our campaign too.

Proverbs chapter 3 verse 5 says:

> Trust in the Lord completely, and do not rely on your own opinions. With all your heart rely on him to guide you, and he will lead you in every decision you make. (TPT)

God knows what we need and when we need it, and I love how He is always working for our good.

The Spirit-led church

1 Kings chapter 19, verse 12, describes God's voice as 'a still, small voice'. God's voice is hidden in the wind, in the rain, in the happy laugh of a friend, in the generous act of a stranger, in the goodness that prevails. He is always speaking to us.

I know that the same God who spoke the stars into being speaks constantly into my heart. Sometimes I may not hear it, but I am wanting to become more aware of His voice every day. To be in communication with the great Creator of the heavens and the earth is such an incredible honour.

When we listen to the voice of God, we start to become Spirit-led as we follow His voice like a shepherd to his sheep. The things we are able to accomplish when we listen to Him are beyond miraculous. The world becomes more beautiful when we start to seek God and hear His voice.

In the busyness of your day, take a moment to listen for His still, small voice. Although the noise of the world may bombard our ears, may we hear Him from our hearts as He calms us and leads us into the beautiful future He has all planned out for each of us.

> And you will seek Me and find Me, when you search for Me with all your heart. (Jeremiah 29:13 NKJV)

THE GATEWAY TO WORSHIP

by Jessica Knell

We all dedicate our lives to worship. Regardless of our professed spirituality, or lack of, our behaviours point to our object of worship.

Our worship extends beyond raised hands in a thirty-minute music performance on a Sunday. Rather, it infiltrates every aspect of our being. Our lives become imprinted by our choice of worship—God, self or others.

Whether we find ourselves engrossed with the pursuit of secular success, or striving to be the most dedicated servant at church, our focus can deviate from worshiping our Holy God.

In the beginning, in Genesis chapter 22, verses 1-10, the concept of worship is introduced. Abraham demonstrated a life of true worship. He worshipped God with fear, obedience and a heart willing to sacrifice all for the glory of God.

As Christians today, how are we to worship God?

Recently I completed a Bible study called Living a Life of True Worship, written by Kay Arthur and Bob and Diane Vereen, whereby I was prompted to examine how the Old Testament tabernacle reveals God calling today for authentic worship.

The Tabernacle

> I am the door; if any one enters through Me, he will be saved and will go in and out and find pasture. (John chapter 10, verse 9 NASB)

When we consider the Christian faith, it appears almost incomprehensible that God longs to have an intimate relationship with us. Yet, He does.

In Exodus chapter 25, God provided Moses with clear instructions on the construction of the tabernacle. The tabernacle was the place where God would meet and communicate with man. Man could approach God in the tabernacle through a process of ritual sacrifice.

God gave the priest specific instructions regarding the process of how and when he could worship God in the tabernacle. The priest did not have the authority to formulate their own way of worship.

Similarly, the function of the tabernacle and the way in which worship took place was required to be done God's way. This practice foreshadowed Jesus and provides us with insight on how we should worship today.

Through reading Exodus chapter 40, we observe that there was only one entrance to the tabernacle—the gateway of the court. Likewise, in John chapter 14, verse 6, it is written that Jesus is the way, truth and life. We are able to have a relationship with God through Jesus—He is the only way. Therefore, apart from Jesus, we are unable to worship God.

Our Advocate

> He Himself is the propitiation for our sins, and not for ours only, but also for those of the whole world. (1 John chapter 2, verse 2 NASB)

How are we, as sinners, to approach our perfect God? Jesus is our Advocate. Moreover, Jesus was the ultimate sacrifice who paid the price for all our sin which is sufficient for all time.

In Hebrews chapter 10, verses 19-23, it is written that we can have confidence that we will enter heaven through the blood of Christ. Jesus is the way, He ended the separation between God and man once and for all. Hence Jesus is our High Priest.

How does this relate to the tabernacle? Well, there are many parallels that we can highlight between entering through the gateway of the court and entering through Jesus. Namely, that there is only one way.

True Worship

> But you are a chosen race, a royal priesthood, a holy nation, a people for God's own possession, so that you may proclaim the excellencies of Him who has called you out of darkness into His marvellous light. (1 Peter chapter 2, verse 9 NASB)

It is written that we are a royal priesthood, bought through salvation, to serve God. Knowing this, our worship begins when we acknowledge God's holiness and understand that our lives belong to Him.

So, as Christians today, how are we to worship God?

In Romans chapter 12, verse 1, it is written that we are to present our bodies as a living sacrifice. May we live in a manner whereby our lives are characterised by the proclamation of the excellencies of God.

HIT SNOOZE AND CHOOSE JOY

by Petro Swart

I am extraordinarily late to the bandwagon, but I recently discovered something revolutionary—the snooze button.

I will be the first to admit that over the last four years at university, I probably took two too many naps. Per day. Though even with all those naps, I never once hit the snooze button. I would set a five-minute timer or throw caution to the wind and hit the repeat on the initial timer. Never snoozed.

Snooze was not exact enough. It would not result in an alarm going off on a number ending in zero or five. I needed control over everything, including the preciseness of my rest.

There was some comfort in the control of my stress, but there was no joy.

Joy = Strength

After returning from exile and repairing the wall around Jerusalem, the Law was read to the Israelites. To encourage the people, Nehemiah said to them:

> ...'This day is holy to the Lord your God; do not mourn or weep.' For all the people wept as they heard the words of the Law. Then he said to them, 'Go your way. Eat the fat and drink sweet wine and send portions to anyone who has nothing ready, for this day is holy to our Lord. And do

not be grieved, for the joy of the Lord is your strength.'
(Nehemiah chapter 8 verses 9-10 ESV)

Their encouragement and their comfort came from the reassurance that the strength to move forward, to heal, and to keep the law was through God's joy.

Nehemiah encouraged them that day not to be bogged down in the pressure of keeping the law. He encouraged them instead to feast, be merry, and understand the comfort that the Law provides.

In their stress and sudden realisation of loss of control, the Israelites were reminded to remain joyful. Joy would give them the strength to remain in control of their obedience to the law.

They were instructed to be joyful—like it was a choice to be made.

Choose joy

Throughout the Bible we are reminded to be joyful, to rejoice always. And again, I say rejoice! If we are to remain joyful always, it makes sense that we, just like the Israelites, will need to choose joy.

It seems somewhat bizarre that joy is a choice, but for that we must understand how it is different from a fleeting emotion.

One of the definitions of joy is that it is 'a state of happiness or felicity'. A state of happiness. In other words, continual happiness. So, God's command to always remain joyful makes sense, because that is what joy is—continual.

Like every other state or feeling in our lives, like feeling rested or satiated, remaining joyful takes work. Joy is intentional and takes a choice.

How to choose joy

Coming back to my snooze button.

In a way I am busier and more stressed now than I was at university. Real adult life is hard. Despite being busier and more stressed, I am more joyful. Joyful because of the snooze button.

The snooze button allows me to start my day a little slower, ease into it instead of jumping out of bed and rushing right away. Even though I cheat the system by setting my alarm ten minutes earlier, starting slow still reduces my stress.

Setting my alarm to allow me to hit the snooze button and wake up slowly is how I choose joy. Starting me morning slow is my way of intentionally choosing joy.

The same way we need to intentionally make time for quiet time, prayer, and community, we need to set up a life that curates joy.

My mind was honestly blown when I realised the depth of joy that the simple action of setting my alarm ten minutes earlier. A simple snooze button and my whole day started with so much peace and continued with exceeding joy.

Your joy

A snooze button, warm cup of tea, worship chapel, phoning your mom. Whatever it is that sets you up for a continual joy, ensure that it remains a consistent part of your life.

I leave you with this, my prayer for you written by Paul himself. Setting yourself up for joy also sets you up for hope—which I would argue leads to more joy. Our God is great like that.

> May the God of hope fill you with all joy and peace as you trust in Him, so that you may overflow with hope by the power of the Holy Spirit. (Romans chapter 15 verse 13 NIV)

DEAR CHILD OF GOD
by Jo Fuller

As I sat down to write a letter to my daughter, thoughts on Freedom were bubbling away in my heart. I knew she wouldn't be able to read it for quite some time or fully grasp the content for many years to come. And when she does read it, I don't know how it will be received or what impact the words may have, but none of that matters as I believe these words are what God wants me to share with her and I believe He will use it for a specific time in her future.

As a parent I have a great love for my children which gives me a tiny insight into the love our heavenly Father has for us and I can only attempt to echo His rich, life-giving words that He has for us; his sons and daughters…

Dear Daughter,

How precious God's thoughts are about you. You are made in His image and you are His masterpiece. He has a good plan for you and your life, and He will work all things together for good.

We need to keep Him number one in our lives; to love him with all our heart and to keep seeking. His word says if we keep seeking, we will find him and if we knock the door will be opened to us (Matthew chapter 7, verse 7). When we accept Jesus as our Lord and choose to follow him and his ways, the most abundant life awaits.

Will it always be easy? Not at all! In fact, persecution for believing in Him is inevitable. So, are we to shrink back and hide away? At times this will be tempting but we are to shine brightly; to live in this world but not be of it.

We can't do it on our own or in our own strength. The Holy Spirit is our great helper, our guide and counsellor but we need to invite him in and be still enough to hear his gentle whisper.

God is merciful, gracious and loving, evidenced by Him sending His son Jesus to willingly die in our place, for our sins. He doesn't just want us to be saved so we can go to heaven one day while we still live in chains here on earth. He wants us to be free from anything that may hold us down, so we can be free to be fully alive in Him. To love Him without reservation and in turn love others.

Freedom From

Precious child of God, His desire is for you to be re-born into freedom.
Freedom from the world and its ways; the distractions, the desires, the earthly mind-sets.
Freedom from Fear; fear of man, fear of failure, fear of the future.

Freedom from Lies; the lies of the enemy, which often attacks our minds and thought life. Which is why it is so crucial to know the Word and the truth.

Freedom from worry, doubt and rejection, envy, jealousy and bitterness.

And freedom from our fleshly selves; self-pity, self-loathing and selfish ambition.

Freedom To

Let's turn our hearts toward Jesus and set our thoughts on things above. May we be free to know our Creator and be fully known by Him.

Free to love Him and serve Him wholeheartedly; to follow Him and His ways.

Freedom to say yes to Him and no to other things that may lead us away from His best.

Free to dance, sing, write, create and dream with our Heavenly Father. Free to embrace and enjoy life.

Does this freedom mean we are free to do whatever we like? To satisfy our fleshly desires. No, for this will only end in heartache and away from the good plan He has for us.

Rather it is a Freedom birthed from grace to be free from anything that is not of Him. Free to embrace our God given identity, authority, rights and privileges as a child of God. Put your trust in Him, and you will be filled with unimaginable love, joy and peace.

THE ARMOUR OF GOD: HELMET OF SALVATION

by Nic Lee

In addition to all this, take up the shield of faith, with which you can extinguish all the flaming arrows of the evil one. Take the helmet of salvation and the sword of the Spirit, which is the word of God.

And pray in the Spirit on all occasions with all kinds of prayers and requests. With this in mind, be alert and always keep on praying for all the Lord's people. (Ephesians chapter 6, verses 16 – 18 NIV)

Praying the helmet of salvation and its truth over people is empowering. May these words of encouragement help to reinforce the truth that God alone is the one who grants us His salvation.

Definition and Significance

The helmet of salvation naturally protects our head and mind. Our salvation acts as a filter in protecting our thoughts because when we have Jesus with us, He perfects our faith and renews our minds. Indeed, the public acceptance of Jesus and His salvation is part of what baptism means—and this symbolises our death to our old ways and transformation into a new, born-again believer.

Prayer

Dear God, I pray for the people who read this article. May they each be reminded of who you are in their lives and that as fellow believers, we share this gift of salvation which comes from You alone. You know each of our hearts and minds, so help us to fill them with Your love and peace.

Specifically, I pray Philippians chapter 4, verse 6-7, over them—that in giving you thanks, they will indeed not be anxious. Help them to lean not on their own understanding but seek Your heart and will for their life. Our minds are indeed a battlefield so we submit this arena to You so that we can know right from wrong and truth from deception. May Your light shine brightly in the darkness of this world; may no one, no word, no thought pass through our minds without being cleansed by You and the saving knowledge that Christ is alive with us via Holy Spirit.

Lord, I pray the helmet of salvation will be a ready and handy tool that you, God, have given us to help connect into Your heavenly peace. Remind us that the helmet represents our salvation, which is You, Christ Jesus.

Help us to consider and reflect on this very nature of the helmet of salvation—that salvation is a gift from You, God, which we cannot earn but have been given freely from Your grace. As we are saved by Your grace and love alone to wear and put on the helmet of salvation simply requires us to acknowledge God and accept Your gift. Lord—we receive Your precious gift right now.

Just as a king may knight and don a helmet on one of his soldiers, I visualise You, Father God, knighting us and placing this helmet of salvation over our heads. As I reflect on this imagery, I also can see You have placed the helmet on our heads as we bow before You, our Heavenly King, You embrace us and provide a heavenly and just kiss on the helmet—it is precious and even though the helmet is an outer covering separate from our own heads, we can feel the touch of Your lips as Your love pours out on impact into the helmet and our own heads.

Let us all wear our helmets securely and know that You, God, bring us peace of mind. Help keep our minds balanced so that we will not be overconfident or boastful of our capability. Instead, help us proclaim confidently the truth of Your salvation over our lives. Jesus, you saved us and nothing can take this away from us.

When we start getting ahead of ourselves, remind us, God, that we are right where You want us to be. You know both our past and future so let us submit it all to you at the foot of the cross so that no fear, doubt or anxious thoughts can take hold. Your Word to the Philippians is simple in instruction, so help us to not overcomplicate issues and simply not be anxious.

Thank you that we have the power to choose how we feel and react in all situations—good or bad. Even more so, during the tough times, help me to proclaim Hallelujah, praise and honour, all to You, God.

In Jesus Name,
Amen.

> Oh that rugged cross, my Salvation
> Where Your love poured out over me
> Now my soul cries out Hallelujah
> Praise and honour unto Thee

(Man of Sorrows, Hillsong Worship, Brook Ligertwood and Matt Crocker)

THE PERFECT WORKOUT

by Jesse Moore

It's a well known fact that eating healthy and exercising regularly keeps people strong and fit, but what about spending time with God? Sure, physical fitness is pretty important, it gives us the ability to do more, provides us with energy and keeps us on top of our game. If physical fitness is this important, imagine what spiritual strength could do for us.

David's mighty warriors

David's Mighty Warriors are the perfect example of strength. Some of the stories told about them in 2 Samuel explain how the Israelite army retreated from battle against the Philistines but Eleazar (one of three Mighty Warriors) stayed behind and defeated the whole army alone. This book even mentions that his hand grew tired and froze to the sword.

To fight off a whole army single handedly this man must have been huge, he would have hit the gym every morning for four hours before eating a breakfast of pure protein to become this strong. While he definitely played a key role in this victory, 2 Samuel chapter 23, verse 10, says at the end of the sentence: 'The Lord brought about a great victory that day'.

Spiritual workout

It's more than likely that Eleazar knew that verse would be written before he even picked up his sword. He knew God would equip him to win the battle. Not only was this man physically strong, he was spiritually strong. I'd say he spent a lot more time with God than he did at the gym and that devotion was the sole factor in the victory.

The fact that the Israelites retreated probably says more about their lack of faith in God than about their ability to defeat the Philistines. If they had the spiritual strength of Eleazar, they could have defeated the enemy 10 times over since it wasn't a matter of how strong they are but how strong their faith is.

The battle is won

Often, we think that we can just work on our relationship with God later and keep pushing it back until we need it, as if God is only useful when we need help. Spending time with God is the spiritual equivalent of going to the gym and eating healthy food so you can have the benefits of living that healthy lifestyle.

On another point, Eleazar didn't stop when he got tired of fighting. As mentioned earlier, his hand froze to the sword as he kept on fighting. I think there is a lot to be said about Eleazar's perseverance in this battle. Often when things get tough, the first thing we feel like doing is quitting but, like Eleazar, we should know that with God, the battle is won before we even pick up our sword.

> He gives strength to the weary and increases the power of the weak. Even youths grow tired and weary, and young men stumble and fall; but those who hope in the Lord will

renew their strength. They will soar on wings like eagles; they will run and not grow weary, they will walk and not be faint. (Isaiah chapter 40, verses 29-31 NIV)

ABOUT THE AUTHORS
(In order of first appearance)

The *God In Life Anthology* is a collection of articles authored by the writers of Press Service International which was established by Dr Mark Tronson in 2005. PSI writers contribute a monthly column which is published in Christian Today Australia's popular online magazine. The PSI writers come from all different walks of life which makes their contributions rich and colourful, whilst distinctly showing their shared love for Christ and the joy of finding God in the everyday journey of the Christian walk.

Dr Mark Tronson

Dr Mark Tronson is a Baptist minister (retired) who served as the Australian cricket team chaplain for 17 years (2000 ret) and established Life After Cricket in 2001. He was recognised by the Olympic Ministry Medal in 2009 presented by Carl Lewis—Olympian of the Century. He mentors young writers and has written 24 books, and enjoys writing. He is married to Delma, with four adult children and grand-children. Dr Tronson writes a daily article for Christian today Australia (since 2008) and in November 2016 established Christian Today New Zealand. Dr Mark Tronson's Press Service International in 2019 was awarded the Australasian Religious Press Association's premier award—The Gutenberg—a great honour.

Elise Pappas
Elise is a Pastor and, together with her husband, pastors a church on the Sunshine Coast in Queensland, Australia. They have a son, Jonathan and a daughter, Sophie. Elise is a former clinical drug trial research coordinator and business owner. She writes about life and ministry experiences.

Araina Kazia Pereira
Araina is from Wellington, New Zealand. She has written for various outlets, most recently as a young writer for Press Service International. She enjoys asking the big questions and writing about the challenging questions that she has wrestled with on her own journey, as well as her learnings along the way.

Jo Fuller
Jo Fuller lives on the beautiful Sunshine Coast with her husband, son and daughter. Jo is a teacher with an education in journalism and early childhood who loves to spend time with her family and enjoys reading and writing whenever she can.

Jessica Knell
Jessica enjoys spending time in nature and reading a good book. Writing is her way of communicating with God, expressing creativity and processing ideas.

Petro Swart
Petro is a recent physical education graduate from the University of Otago. Originating from South Africa and growing up in New Zealand has given Petro a love for all things sport and travel. Writing is Petro's way of making sense of the world around her and expressing the words God places on her heart.

Joseph F. Kolapudi

Joseph Kolapudi is a third-culture-kid born in Australia to Indian parents, and returned from California where he was studying theology at Fuller; currently, he is working with a missions agency and continuing his love of writing by contributing to PSI.

Neville Hiatt

Nevill spent a decade working for radio stations before his career was intermissioned by someone in a hurry to get home from work. He now runs a blog www.nevillehiatt.com where he shares his desire to Inspire, Create, Motivate, and Educate through his photography, poetry and short stories. He occasionally blogs for www.altcoincollege.com covering the way cryptocurrencies and blockchain are changing our world.

Amy Manners

Amy is a Press Service International columnist from Adelaide. She holds a BA in Media and Creative Writing and is a freelance photographer, videographer and writer. Nature is her cathedral.

Nic Lee

Nic works by day as a Business Analyst Consultant whilst, outside of business hours, maintains an IT support and website services business. He volunteers with 89.9 Light FM (Christian Community Radio). Nic has served for over twenty years in his local church, in the areas of worship, technology consulting, life group leading and event management.

Russell Modlin

Russell teaches English and Physical Education at a Christian School on the Sunshine Coast, QLD. He is married to Belinda and they have three children.

Esther Koh
Esther Koh is a stay-at-home mum living in Wellington with her husband and two sons. She loves people and has a passion for helping others find their purpose for living.

Jesse Moore
Jesse lives on the Sunshine Coast, Qld, and is studying a double degree: a Bachelor of Arts in Screen and Media, and a Bachelor of Business in Marketing. He draws from the Bible and classical literature for insight into life's tough questions.

John Skinner
John served as an infantry soldier in Vietnam then the Tasmanian Police before taking up the position of CEO of the Australian Rough Riders Association (professional rodeo based in Warwick Qld). Before retirement to his small farm, he was a photo-journalist for 25 years. He is married with three children and seven grandchildren.

Rebecca Howan
Rebecca is from Wellington, New Zealand, where she works as an Executive Assistant in the humanitarian sector. She worships and serves at The Salvation Army, and is passionate about music, travelling the world and building community.

Kevin Park
Kevin is studying at Carey Baptist College and finds that Christian writing is his ultimate will of God and his ultimate method to build the Kingdom of God. He started to become a Christian writer in 2013. Other than his writing life, Kevin desires to see that each finds everlasting satisfaction in God, the Almighty. He loves to encourage others spiritually.

Matthew Thornton
Matthew is studying at the University of Auckland and finds that writing is one of the prime ways he connects with and grows closer to God. He loves seeing the way in which God has wired everyone uniquely and finds immense fulfilment in seeing others discover who God is to them.

Jessica McPherson
Jessica McPherson lives with her best friend and husband, Eoin and their family of rescue animals in Christchurch. She loves reading, writing, photography and scrapbooking but most of all sharing God's love and truth with a hurting world. Jessica is particularly passionate about encouraging children and building them up in gospel truth.

Kristen Dang
Kristen is a family doctor, and author of the e-book, An Internship with Jesus. She lives with her husband and daughter in Adelaide and writes a regular blog (lostnowfoundk) on life with God. Her second blog (lilyofthevalleysk), aims to share her love for Jesus through the creative arts.

Rebecca Moore
Rebecca and her husband have four children and live on the Sunshine Coast, Australia. Rebecca writes for various publications including print, online and commercial. She is the author of two books: 'First to Forty' and 'Pizza and Choir'. For more information you can find Rebecca at: http://www.rebeccamoore.life, Facebook: Rebecca Moore - Author, Instagram: rebeccamoore_author

Blake Gardiner
Hailing from North Auckland, Blake Gardiner sounds American, looks Swedish, but grew up in Laos. As an

introvert, Blake lives life on the edge by socialising. When he isn't putting his life at such risk, he enjoys reading theology and debating whether Interstellar is truly the greatest movie of all time.

Cartia Moore
Cartia Moore is a sword fighter, trained and skilled in the art of fencing. She has recently graduated from her Bachelor of Arts degree and has completed an Honours in Screen & Media Studies. She is now going on to do a Master of Teaching (Secondary), focusing in the teaching areas of English and Film studies. She is passionate and driven to inspire and encourage others to seek and find their worth and value in Him.

Manuele Teofilo
Manuele lives in South Auckland with his parents and siblings. He has graduated from the University of Auckland with a Bachelor of Human Services and plans to work in the disability sector. He enjoys getting around in his electric wheelchair and having fun with people.

Roydon Ng
Roydon is a Christian writer from Western Sydney, a former Sydney Morning Herald journalist with a diploma of Ministry from Morling College.

Jeremy Dover
Jeremy is a Sports Scientist, Author and former Pastor. He has been part of SCA for over 20 years and served as sports chaplain in soccer, track and field and triathlon. He has served as Victoria SCA Coordinator, Training Coordinator and National Office Manager.

David Goodwin

David Goodwin is the former Editor of The Salvation Army's magazine, War Cry. He is also a cricket tragic, and an unapologetic geek.

Travis Barnes

Travis Barnes lives in central Victoria with his wife and two daughters. He is a contributor for Christian Today and a sportswriter.

You can find Press Service International Writers online at:

 www.pressserviceinternational.org
 facebook.com/AusCTyoungwriters
facebook.com/ausCTseniorwriters
 instagram.com/aus_youngwriters

www.ingramcontent.com/pod-product-compliance
Lightning Source LLC
Chambersburg PA
CBHW071858290426
44110CB00013B/1201